BASS
PRO STRATEGIES

Locating And Catching Techniques
Of The Professionals

by Larry Larsen

Book III in the Bass Series Library
by Larsen's Outdoor Publishing

ISBN 0-936513-01-2

Library of Congress 87-82757

Published by:

LARSEN'S OUTDOOR PUBLISHING
2640 Elizabeth Place
Lakeland, FL 33813

PRINTED IN THE UNITED STATES OF AMERICA

4 5 6 7 8 9 10

DEDICATION

To my father, Floyd, who has, from the beginning of my life, taught me to be the best that I can. He'll always be a Pro in my mind.

ACKNOWLEDGMENTS

I wish to acknowledge the contribution of many persons in the development of this book. Firstly, my gratitude goes to wife, Lilliam, for her valuable assistance and editorial eye on this endeavor. Sincere thanks go to all of the professional bass anglers quoted within the covers of the book. I have shared a boat with all but one or two, and they are indeed professionals. Each is a great angler from whom I have learned.

Deserving of my gratitude for their support of my efforts, both magazine and books, are the many magazine editors and publishers, and newspaper columnists. They have truly motivated me in my literary endeavors. My deepest appreciation, though, goes to the interested bass fishermen everywhere that seek to improve their abilities at catching bass.

PREFACE

All anglers strive to become more proficient at their sport. That is easily achieved by some through careful study of outdoor magazines and fishing books, and then, through practice and on-the-water experience. For many, that can take quite a while.

Few anglers can afford to spend huge amounts of time at their hobby. Those that can devote a couple of hundred days each year to their bass fishing interests are usually professional fishermen. Guides, touring tournament anglers, TV fishing show personalities and an occasional outdoor writer have opportunities to devote extended amounts of time to the sport of bass fishing.

The vast majority of anglers must be satisfied with two or three trips per month perhaps. They can, however, learn from the professionals—those anglers making a living on the water. Pros don't last long in the business unless they can learn from their vast experiences and apply that knowledge to catching more fish the next time out.

They are usually adept at analyzing a body of water and planning a productive day on it. They know how changes in pH and water temperature, color and fluctuation affect bass fishing, and they know how to adapt to weather variations. Most of the more successful pros are structure fishermen who have intimate knowledge of topographical influences to the location of bass. They can find and catch the fish.

"BASS PRO STRATEGIES" reveals the methods that the country's most successful tournament anglers have employed to catch bass almost every time out. The reader's productivity should improve after spending a few hours with this compilation of techniques!

CONTENTS

ABOUT THE AUTHOR

A writer about bass fishing for more than 16 years, Larry Larsen has studied all aspects of the fish, and the ways to catch them. The author's articles and photography frequently appears in *Outdoor Life*, *Sports Afield*, *Fishing Facts*, and *Field & Stream*. More than 700 of Larsen's magazine articles on bass fishing have been published in 50 different publications, including *Bassin'*, *Bassmaster*,

Larry Larsen and one of his fishing adventures

Bass Illustrated, U.S. Bass, Petersen's Fishing, and other major outdoor magazines. He has been honored with several regional and national awards over the years for both outdoor writing and photography.

Larry Larsen has literally traveled the world to fish for bass. He has fished lakes near the Canadian border; in Honduras' Lake Yojoa; Cuba's Treasure Lake; and the plantation lakes in the Hawaiian Islands. Larsen's fishing adventures have taken him to nearly every State, where he has often fished with other professional anglers.

Bass anglers of any skill level that apply the information contained within these covers will greatly benefit. The book details productive tricks and tactics that any angler, novice or professional, can apply to catch more bass. Numerous photographs and figures help detail productive methods.

His first two books "Follow The Forage For Better Bass Angling" and "Shallow Water Bass," were acclaimed by outdoor scribes throughout the country and continue to be a big success with bass anglers everywhere. He is a member of the Outdoor Writers Association of America (OWAA), the Southeastern Outdoor Press Association (SEOPA), and the Florida Outdoor Writers Association (FOWA) and is a graduate of Wichita State University and Colorado State University.

WHAT OTHERS HAVE SAID ABOUT LARSEN
AND HIS BOOKS

"The author stands head and shoulders above other writers."
—Jerry Hill, Bradenton Herald

"Larsen writes more on bass fishing than any other writer."
—Charley Dickey, Tallahassee Democrat

"Better Bass Angling" . . .

". . . is one of the most informative books on bass fishing that I've read in the 80's."
—Charles Salter, Atlanta Journal

". . . is one of the most complete books available on the subject."
—*Outdoor Life*

". . . a splash with the growing fraternity of bass anglers."
—Colin Moore, Pensacola News Journal

". . . is the best how-to book to come off the press in years."
—Johnny Pate, DeFuniak Springs Herald

". . . fills the void of books on bass behavior."
—David Dunaway, Gainesville Sun

". . . is a studious, meticulous approach to help you increase your success."
—Michael Levy, Buffalo News

". . . gets to the meat of the matter."
—Ben Callaway, Philadelphia Inquirer

". . . is a technical study of bass forage as the key to catching more largemouths."
—Frank Sargeant, Tampa Tribune

". . . is 358 pages of bass lore gleaned from the nation's top scientists, recognized bass experts and lifetime of study on the part of Larsen."

—Jerry Hill, Bradenton Herald

". . . will increase your knowledge, whether you are a serious tournament angler or a fun fisherman."

—Del Milligan, Lakeland Ledger

". . . explores the forage-bass relationship in full."

—Russell Tinsley, Austin Statesman

". . . is loaded with information Larsen has accumulated in years of fishing for the wily bass."

—Henry Reynolds,
Memphis Commercial Appeal

". . . is a valuable book which I guarantee will help you understand what's going on down there where your lure is."

—Jim Spencer, Pine Bluff Commercial

"Shallow Water Bass"

". . . is the first book ever published that identifies particular methods that can be systematically applied to locate bass in shallow water."

—*Bassin' Magazine*

". . . is especially relevant for fishermen who do most of their angling in water less than 10 feet deep."

—Frank Sargeant, Tampa Tribune

". . . presents concepts which the bass angler should be able to apply to his home waters."

—Byron Stout, Ft. Myers News Press

". . . helps the fisherman to develop a systematic approach to consistently locate bass."

—Bill Sargent, Florida Today

". . . offers a lot for the novice, as well as for the tournament angler."

—Richard Bowles, Gainesville Sun

". . . offers tips and guides to increase both your strikes and actual landings of bass."

—Jerry Hill, Bradenton Herald

INTRODUCTION

PROFESSIONAL BASS FISHING STRATEGIES

CATCHING LARGEMOUTH BASS consistently requires lots of knowledge, hard work and, at times, maybe even a little luck. Few anglers are as productive day after day as are the professional fishermen that spend over 200 days on the water annually. Their experiences are vast, and each relies upon in-depth knowledge gained over many such years.

The professional bass angler who travels the country fishing various bodies of water learns to develop a sense about what technique will be effective under the conditions found on each lake or river. That strategy development is the key to their success and longevity as pros. Without that ability, they won't last long. They won't attract industry sponsors for their tournament activities and they won't become heros to the weekend anglers that dream of someday going "pro on the tournament trail."

It's the better ones that this book focuses on. Top professional anglers achieve such status because they are productive when it counts. Their strategies on how largemouth are found and then caught are the keys to their development in a field that's loaded with competition. This book is a study of some of their secrets to success.

Through the experiences of several of these top professionals, as well as my own, I have tried to cover the essentials in developing a sound strategy to, first, plan the productive fishing trip, and then to carry out the objective. Part I of **"BASS PRO STRATEGIES"** discusses the planning and analysis necessary to know what should be done ahead of time.

The Focus

Interpretation and use of topo maps are the beginning to the study. Then the pro advice turns to water elimination. Bass are concentrated in only a small portion of the water available and knowing how to quickly eliminate the vast, potentially unproductive areas is one of the keys to catching more fish.

An analysis of shallow water systems and deep water systems is the next step to finding more bass. Being adept at marking the concentrations of bass found, while not revealing it to others is paramount to success in areas of extreme fishing pressure. Use of buoys, natural markers and "hidden" markers is delineated.

Then into the boat we must go for some important lessons on boat control and positioning for maximum catches from the bow casting platform. The backseat angler also gets excellent advice from the pros on catching bass when relegated to the rear casting pedestal. Knowing who, or rather what, to compete with is the key to doing well there.

Part II discusses how the pros adapt to conditions at the lake or river that they are fishing. What they find in the way of water quality, weather and topography dictates how they will approach the task of catching bass. These location factors and their meanings are the puzzle that each angler must solve every time out.

Monitoring pH and water level changes are vital to many professionals' successes; so is utilizing visibility limitations affected by water color changes. The professionals easily understand what seems like complicated topics but are not. Any angler should be able to catch more bass from studying the three chapters on water changes.

Weather factors such as temperature, wind and frontal clouds can influence the location of bass concentrations. Professionals must deal with the problems encountered under a variety of changing weather throughout the year. Tournament anglers must fish when the events are scheduled, regardless of the current weather conditions.

The final three chapters of **"BASS PRO STRATEGIES"** deal with bass and their relationship to topography. Variations to natural bottom and vegetation structures impact where bass concentrations will move. And, when bass are not on structure, they are tough-to-catch suspended fish. The pros reveal their secrets on unlocking the jaws of off-structure largemouth.

16

The Pros

The professionals offering their advice and insights within the covers of this book are tops in their field. All are effective at not only finding and catching fish under all conditions, but also at educating others on their effective strategies. Sharing their knowledge with us are several notables.

Rick Clunn should need no introduction. The all-time money leader in professional tournament fishing has done it all. A multiple winner of the Bass Masters Classic and the U.S. Open, the Montgomery, Texas pro has competed successfully on several tournament trails and usually is at the top in prestige/big money events.

Hemphill, Texas seems to produce great professional competitors. Larry Nixon and Tommy Martin are two outstanding anglers who have each amassed impressive credentials along the various tournament trails. Nixon has won more that a dozen major bass events and probably has the second highest accumulated winnings in professional bass fishing. Bass Master Classic winner Martin has qualified for that event more than anyone through consistent placing in the top ten at major tournaments.

Harold Allen, now of Batesville, Mississippi, is a former Toledo Bend guide out of Hemphill. He has established a super successful career by always doing well on the major tournament circuits. Denny Brauer of Camdenton, Missouri turned "pro" half a dozen years ago and has probably won as much money in major events as anyone since.

Ken Cook of Meers, Oklahoma is a big name on the various tournament trails, for good reason. Part of the credit to his consistent performance in all professional events goes to the former biologist's knowledge of bass and their interaction to water quality and chemistry.

Randy Fite, of Montgomery, Texas, is a top competitor on the tournament trail and is a leading authority on the use of sonar equipment in bass fishing. TV outdoor show host, Ron Shearer from Hardin, Kentucky consistently places high in professional events, as does Woo Daves from Chester, Virginia and Charlie Ingram of Columbia, Tennessee.

The contingent of professionals who reveal strategies that have worked often for them include regular Bass Masters Classic competitors Rayborn Waits, of Austin, Texas; 1987 winner George Cochran of North Little Rock, Arkansas; Gary Klein of Oroville, California; and Larry Williams, of Lakeview, Ohio.

Numerous photographs and figures are used throughout the book to graphically illustrate many of the techniques and strategies revealed in the text. Such extensive use should aid the reader in developing a clear understanding of the concepts.

CHAPTER 1

MAPPING LORE

Significant Information From Topo Maps

SUCCESSFUL BASS FISHING strategies can be determined from topographical maps, if you know what to look for. Indeed, many of the professional bass tournament anglers are very adept at such 'analyses'. A touring pro is frequently faced with waters that are new to him. It is usually impossible for an angler to fish on all waters in one state, let alone in the country.

Many anglers travel extensively throughout the United States and fish several bass tournament circuits. While visiting each tournament site on their schedule, they put thousands of miles on their trailers. When they get to the lakes, they don't necessarily want to do the same to their boats.

Professionals like Larry Nixon, Harold Allen, Randy Fite, and Ron Shearer want to minimize travel on-the-water and develop productive, bass-catching patterns quickly. They usually do this by utilizing an important 'tool,' that being a topographical map of the waters. Each of these anglers place a lot of value in a good 'topo' map, as they are normally called.

Larry Nixon feels that the most important time to use a topo map is the time of year when the fish are on drops or breaks. The Hemphill, Texas guide and tournament pro looks for contour lines that come extremely close together. The winner of several big-money tournaments has had many successes on unfamiliar waters around the country, thanks to his ability to interpret topo lines.

Tight Lines

"The closest contour lines on a map describe the sharpest drop points and the areas that fish usually relate to," says Nixon. "When you have a good idea as to the depth and type of water the bass are holding in, you can develop a good pattern using a topo map."

"It doesn't have to be a great depth change, just anywhere those contour lines come together and provide a change—at the back of a pocket, or out on a point," he explains. "Even the smallest amount of change, like from three to six feet, if it's a sharp drop, will hold concentrations of bass. On points, I look for a channel coming near to the shallows."

"When lakes are cleared, the cutting crews avoid the hard to get to areas, or just saw off trees they can reach, leaving stumps," says Nixon. "Bass relate to these changes. On roadbeds, points, underwater bridges, fencelines, or old tree rows, bass will relate to the change in the bottom, wherever the sharpest dropoff occurs."

Bass professional Larry Nixon feels that the most important time of year to use a topo map is when the bass are on the drops or breaks in deep water.

"There might be a road ditch paralleling the treeline and an old creek crossing the ditch," adds Nixon. "Usually that type of area is the place your looking for on topo maps."

A topo map will show you the coves and creeks that have definite channels, which Nixon feels is very important in the springtime when you're looking for concentrations of fish. The pro seeks out such breaks that may offer a migration route to the bass. A flat cove or pocket without a channel in it will have very few fish, normally according to Nixon.

"Flat areas can be good in the spring though," he says. "Areas with lines that are greatly separated are often spawning flats. The good maps will reveal little ditches or ridges in the flat areas and there might be more than 10 or 15 fish concentrated there," Nixon points out. "A large flat area that makes for a good spawning ground may have a ditch or channel that leads to outside drops or ridges near, and even more fish may be concentrated in such an area."

Seasonal Considerations

Harold Allen agrees, "The majority of bigger fish spawn in deeper water. After the spawn, they migrate to the outside of the

Harold Allen studies his topo maps for something that's different, that's not so obvious. His tournament success proves that such analyses are worthwhile.

21

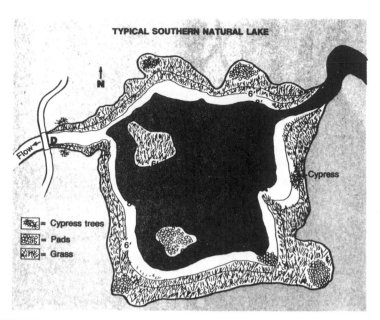

FIGURE 1—*Contour lines are found even on topo maps of shallow southern natural lakes. Following the deeper lines to a point where excellent structure exists will mean numerous bass opportunities.*

flat," he says. "They're going to bunch up on points and knolls. When they're in the shallows they'll be scattered out, but on a point they'll be bunched," Allen explains. "That's what I look for when reading a topo map."

"When they move out to these points, they may not be hitting, so you'll have to fish grubs or small lures," advises the Batesville, Mississippi, professional. "When they get active crankbaits will get them. The average fisherman, though, is going to stay in and keep pounding the banks."

"The time of year is the main thing that tells us what to look for on a topo map," says Allen. "Knowing the time of year, we'll try to dissect the map," he says. "Deeper water just off the flats could be a good post-spawn or early-spawn area."

"If a channel comes near a change in depth, bass will use that for the summertime activity," he adds. "The bends in a deep channel are always good. The outside bends are slightly deeper than the inside bends, and they'll probably have more brush."

"A depth finder comes in handy to sort this out. Bass move up and down a channel, until they find the kind of water that's good for them. The depth is constantly changing. A fish will look for something different along a break. The best areas are a combination of good structure, deep water and flats."

"I look for some little area that's different, that's not so obvious," says Allen. "That's your edge if any. That's really not hard to find on a map."

"We can select the areas that look good on a topo map, but what kills us is the time it takes to check them out once we're on the water," he observes. "There could very well be something on that map that doesn't show, like a little ditch that cuts across a point. The fish could be stacked in that depression."

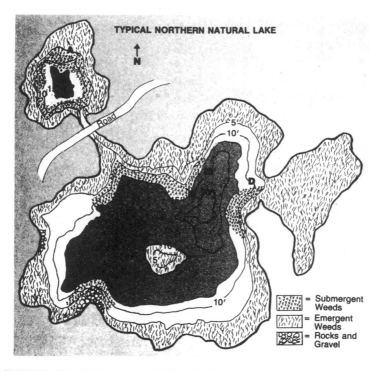

FIGURE 2—*The depth of natural lakes in the northern areas may be depicted by contour lines that are closer together, but the same keys to success should be noticed on any waters.*

23

"If we fish deep structure, we've got to run in and fish the obvious stuff that the bank chunkers are fishing too," notes Allen. "In the limited time that we have, we also have to fish the obvious deep water structure found on the topo maps."

Coloring The Lines

Randy Fite is well known for his bass locating abilities. The Montgomery, Texas guide and professional fisherman is an expert at interpreting flashers and graphs, and topo maps. He believes that choosing the right map is extremely important.

"Always get the best available, one that has the best contour lines on it," he advises. "Sometimes, I'll color those contour lines so that at a glance, it is very easy to see each."

Fite explains why. "Once you get on a lake and develop a pattern, such as the fish are at 25 foot and holding on sharp breaks, you can pull out the map and follow the 25-foot contour line until it comes closest to a 40-foot contour line, for example. That will be a sharp, vertical drop from the crest of 25-foot water and a good area! If the lines are color-coded, that will help speed up the process of finding a similar location."

"As far as looking for particular structures on topo maps, you have to keep in mind your seasonal patterns," he says. "Summer structures appear relatively flat or gradually sloping. On the map, I'll look for lines that are far apart."

"In the winter time, I'll look for steep, vertical drops, and the topo contour lines for these places will be very close together. You'll usually find that structure around the major creek channels or out on the major river channels," advises Fite. "Those will be better in cold water situations."

Irregular Features

Professional bass angler and TV show host Ron Shearer is a firm believer in the value of topo maps. When visiting a new lake, the

Randy Fite believes in getting the best contour map available and then when on the water, using his electronic depth finders to pin point the areas that he has selected to fish.

very first thing to do, he believes, is to sit down and pick out the irregular features of a map.

"I've yet to see a summer tournament that wasn't won structure fishing," comments Shearer. "Structure is any irregular feature on the bottom or on the bank. The best summer time structure is usually out in the middle of the lake, and topo maps will help you find it."

"I have never seen a hot-weather tournament that you couldn't just lay a map down and notice that the spot where it was won, was like a 'blinking' light," says Shearer. "That's always the case!"

Any time Shearer visits a lake, he'll order a good topographical map from the Corps. of Engineers. He will sit down and study it. The more that you look at it and get familiar with it, the better off you are, according to the Hardin, Kentucky, professional angler. You'll know what to expect.

"Often you can't be ready to catch the fish until you know what's there," says Shearer. "A map can reveal detail about the area that would take a while to find out on the water. The first thing that I look for is contour lines that are close together with fingers sticking out or indentions coming in. Then, I'll figure out how deep it is."

"I remember one time I marked all the fingers on a topo map that didn't have the depths noted on it. When I got to the lake, about half of them were out of the water, on ridge tops," Shearer laughs. "You also have to know the depth so that you don't mark creek channels that are 125 feet deep!"

"Learning to use topographical maps is by far the easiest way to catch fish. Catching bass is like building a puzzle," he explains further. "The map gives you an outline—the edge pieces—so that you can put the rest of it together."

CHAPTER 2

WATER ELIMINATION

Quick Steps To Cull Unproductive Areas

THE TOURNAMENT PROFESSIONAL is regularly challenged by unfamiliar waters. Huge impoundments seemingly offer an endless variety of potential bass haunts.

Faced with overwhelming choices of habitat and prospective patterns, the successful touring angler has to be able to 'limit' his fishing time to the most productive areas and methods. There is little time to experiment with various lures or to thoroughly check out a vast number of locations during practice. In fact, few professionals 'guess right' about a spot and technique quickly. All agree that time is well spent by eliminating the majority of water with which they'll be faced.

The angler that most effectively 'culls' acres of water has a good chance at winning the tournament. Quick steps to eliminating the unproductive areas are what separates the successful professionals from most other contenders in a tournament situation. Knowing some of those ways should benefit the weekend angler, or anyone for that matter, who spends limited time on a large body of water.

Tournament winners like Ken Cook, Ron Shearer, Tommy Martin, Rick Clunn and Woo Daves have learned how to effectively eliminate water. They make wise use of valuable time when they are exposed to waters relatively new to them around the country. They've learned to concentrate their practice time on potentially productive habitat. They are constantly learning, whether they catch fish or not. The road to a tournament title takes such abilities.

Water Quality And Habitat

"I look for what seems the best bass holding habitat in the lake," says Cook. "I often fall back to less quality habitat, though, if the best is too obvious and gets all the fishing pressure."

Cook considers type of cover, water color and chemistry such as pH and temperature in his elimination (and selection) process. His Multi-C-Lector, which identifies water pH, temperature and clarity values, is a significant part of that process. Waters with visibility outside an optimal range of 15 to 24 inches will normally be culled.

Good habitat, such as trees, bushes, rocks, grass and drop-offs, is necessary, he believes, but maybe more importantly, it means good water quality. Water that is not too clear and not too muddy is ideal.

Water without a 'greenish' tint is also usually eliminated by Cook. The 'greenish' color guarantees a good base for the food chain, according to the former fisheries biologist. And, since bass are the top predator in this chain, it's necessary to have a good base to produce much at the top. Waters with either consistently too low or too high pH values are also eliminated.

"Once I've eliminated most areas of the lake and settled on the one that I believe to be best, I start fishing and evaluating the available cover types," says Cook. "I look for the type that the bass are preferring at the time, with emphasis on the not-too-obvious cover," he says. "My basic goal is to quickly eliminate cover types that don't hold fish."

Concentration Cover

Ron Shearer also looks for places that are conducive to holding concentrations of largemouth. The pro doesn't wish to spend a lot of time fishing a spot where he can't catch a school of bass. He's not fond of constantly moving about to pick up an isolated bass or two.

Water that is an obvious place to catch only one or two fish, like logs scattered along a bank, is quickly eliminated by Shearer. Most people will go in and catch a couple of bass from that cover, and nothing more. Those places do not hold a concentration of bass, and the anglers have not really established a good pattern.

"I try to eliminate as many places as I can that will not hold a school of bass," he says. "If the water color in a creek, for example, is terrible, revealing the pH is off and bass are inactive, I'll move on. Too, if you're on a gin-clear lake and it's time for the bass to be out on the ledges, you have to cull those creeks."

The bearded Kentuckian will have several back-up spots in mind, though, those holding only a bass or two, when tournament day rolls around. During practice rounds, he'll establish the productive holes and also look the lake over for other obvious fish spots. He likes to know where they are, so that his tournament time can be utilized efficiently if he finds the practice holes are unproductive.

Rick Clunn eliminates three-fourths of the lake before he even sees it, due to seasonal patterns. He sectionalizes a lake, and then relies on his seasonal patterns to put him in its most productive area for that time of year.

"As an example, in the fall, my seasonal patterns tell me to concentrate on the backs of the creeks, preferably the major creeks," Clunn says. "Now, all I have to worry about when I get to the lake are those areas. That gives me a much better chance of locating bass

Rick Clunn will 'sectionalize' a map. Then, he'll concentrate on his seasonal patterns developed over years of experience.

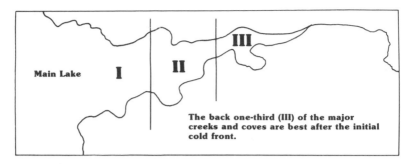

FIGURE 3—*Rick Clunn's intimate knowledge of seasonal patterns helps him eliminate the front two-thirds of a major creek or cove during a fall cold front, for example.*

in a limited amount of time than if I went to the lake with the intention of fishing 20,000 acres!"

Pattern Establishment

Tommy Martin feels that there are no shortcuts to eliminate water. A pattern has to be developed quickly first, he contends.

"Once you establish a pattern and determine the depth of water, type of cover, and clarity of water that you are catching bass in, you can then begin to quickly eliminate areas of the lake that probably won't produce any bass, at least not on the pattern that you have established."

"Keep in mind, though," Martin warns, "there can be a number of patterns or ways to catch bass within a given day. On most lakes during tournaments, I try to establish at least two and sometimes three patterns using different lures. If one plays out, I have something else to go to."

"The only way I feel really satisfied in eliminating water is to fish that water with several different lures," says Martin. "I'll use fast-moving lures, such as crankbaits and spinnerbaits, so I can cover water faster. I'll fish until I'm satisfied there aren't enough bass in the area to catch."

Martin will always stop and fish key cover with a worm or a jig, though, depending on water temperature. He wants to see if there are bass in the area that wouldn't strike a fast moving lure.

Blue Sky Analysis

The professional angler, from Hemphill, Texas, also feels that he can often quickly eliminate water by flying over a lake. He looks for water color differences and depth variations. Martin will cull those areas that are either extremely shallow or muddy.

"One of the most important and fastest means of water elimination is to take an airplane ride over the body of water you are fish-

Once Clunn climbs behind the console, he is prepared to quickly eliminate unproductive waters.

Tommy Martin relies on fast moving lures, such as spinnerbaits, when he's trying to cover and eliminate a lot of water.

ing," agrees Woo Daves. "You can see so much from the air that can be very helpful, even on your home lake."

He will look at the water conditions (clear, stained, muddy) and then for the type of cover he's comfortable fishing. There is usually a lot of dead water in lakes and rivers that you can spot from the air in a hurry, according to the Chester, Virginia pro. If a lake has clear, stained, and muddy water, he prefers to fish in the stained, or on the breakline where stained or muddy water meets clear.

"Next, I look for the right temperature," he adds. "In the spring, the warmest water usually produces best; in summer it's the coolest. Many times in the spring I've seen just a couple of degrees make all the difference between a big catch and nothing."

On strange lakes, Daves looks for the type of cover that he's used to fishing. Usually a pattern can be established. Find the cover you like to fish with the right color water and temperature, and you are in business, he advises.

In the spring, he will concentrate on the larger feeder creeks starting at the mouth and working back. In summer, Daves will fish main lake points and underwater structure. In the fall, he'll move back to major feeder creeks, and then as the weather cools, fish the smaller creeks.

Another key point in water elimination is to look for baitfish, according to Daves. Generally, if there are a lot of baitfish in area, bass will be there also. He once fished Kerr Reservoir and found the water color, temperature and cover the same, but one particular area was holding a lot of baitfish.

"We could fish one creek for 10 minutes, catch five or eight bass, leave to fish identical cover (except without baitfish) for an hour or two and only catch one or two fish," says Daves. "This lasted for two days. We caught over 50 bass in one creek, while we caught only four bass outside of the creek even though we fished the exact places we had caught bass on past trips."

"Before going to a new lake I try to get a good topo map and study it, call local fishermen to get their input, and read any articles I can find on the lake," says Daves. "The more you know before you get there, the quicker you can pinpoint the fish."

It's just like taking a test in school; the more you study the better you're going to do, according to Daves.

CHAPTER 3

SHALLOW WATER SYSTEMS

Special Location Techniques

SHALLOW WATER BASS lakes are found throughout the country. Most states have their share of the 'bass factories.' In fact, the best largemouth fisheries are composed of waters with extensive shallows. It has been said that 90 percent of all largemouth are pulled from waters less than ten feet deep.

I, like a lot of anglers, place a lot of emphasis on 'thin' water and the techniques that are very effective there. Most of the anglers that I know, both weekend fishermen and the guides and tournament pros, spend hours of each angling day in the shallows. Many catch bass, lots of them.

Experts are often successful in waters that they could stand in and still breathe. The professionals know what to look for in the shallows, and more importantly, the special techniques, lures, and boat positioning required to maximize the strikes. They are usually aware of how the weather variables and topographical changes affect the largemouth in his favorite environment.

"Shallow water is where most every person begins and learns to fish for black bass," says professional bass angler, Rayborn Waits. "The only thing needed in shallow water is brush, stumps, rocks, or any other object that bass can relate to, and most of all, a little water color," he says. "The water doesn't have to be muddy. If your white bait disappears in 18 inches of water, you have good color."

There are probably more fish caught from two to five foot depths than all other depths combined, according to Waits. He feels that there's a very simple reason for this. More people fish these depths, objects can be seen and can be fished easier and faster, and last but not least, shallow water bass are catchable bass.

"When I go to a strange lake, the first thing I do is put the boat on a plane and cruise the shallow banks looking for logs, stumps, brush, rock outcroppings, or some kind of vegetation," says Waits.

Brush Patterns

Some of the most consistent bass producing places for the Austin, Texas, pro are large scattered logs that have been in the same place for a long time. They will produce for years, time after time, especially if one end is in one foot of water and the other is in a little deeper, say three feet.

The best way to fish these logs, according to Waits, is to approach them from the deep end and keep the boat about 20 feet off the structure. Cast a spinnerbait to the shallow end and work the lure along both sides out to deeper water. Then, let the spinnerbait fall at the end of the log.

"This method will usually produce an active bass, especially early or late, or on a cloudy day," advises Waits. "But on a blue bird day with no wind, you usually have to work a worm or 1/8 ounce jig & frog slowly along both sides and the end."

"This pattern is best on scattered logs, not log jams; maybe on a log along every 1/2 mile of bank with no other cover around," he says. "I have caught as many as nine bass off the end of one log and never had to move the boat," laughs Waits.

Finding fish in shallow water brush is harder to do, according to Waits. The water level must have been low long enough for small trees and bushes to grow before the level rose and covered the brush. It's harder to find fish in this water, he believes, because there is so much of it.

"The places to concentrate on are the points and at the edges of creeks," he says. "Try flipping the jig at the edge of brush in creeks and try other types of baits along the points."

Weeds And Wind

Fishing shallow water grass, moss, or other weeds is also a

The author has based his successful fishing/writing career on effectively fishing the shallows. Shallow water structure often includes brush, vegetation, logs and bass.

matter of elimination, according to Waits. You can fish a mile of moss beds and there probably won't be more than two small stretches that hold fish. He tries to stay away from the obvious places, such as dips and points, because they get fished a lot.

"I prefer to idle my boat down a straight stretch and watch my depth finder. There will usually be a small stretch that will have a little deeper water," says Waits. "Even a foot difference can hold a good concentration of bass."

"When fish are feeding there, they can be caught on the edge with a number of baits," he says, "but I will often use a one-ounce slip sinker and rig a straight tail worm Texas-style. I'll toothpick the sinker against the head of the worm and flip it into the thickest mass of grass."

This method is deadly at times in the middle of the summer, according to Waits. Just be sure you have heavy line and a stiff rod.

Another way to catch bass in shallow water, where you don't have very much of the aforementioned, is described by Waits. First, locate the roughest banks you can find, where wind and wave erosion has occurred, then fish them. In such areas, when the wind is up and the day is cloudy, Waits has found that tossing buzz baits or shallow crank baits can be very productive.

Waits casts into the wind or upcurrent, bringing the bait back with the current or wind direction. That's important since bass face into the current and wind when feeding.

Water Visibility

Successfully fishing shallow water usually requires muddy water and lots of cover, according to bass angling professional Ken Cook. The man has had more than his share of success on the shallows of tournament waters. He feels that both cover and off-color water will allow a closer approach to bass without spooking them.

Cook relies on two baits most of the time in this situation. His first choice is often a big Colorado blade spinnerbait, usually the 1/2 ounce model with a #5 or #7 blade. He'll make short, accurate casts to every piece of cover in the shallows. Many strikes come as the bait is falling.

"The pull-and-drag is usually the best retrieve unless the water is cold, less than 55 degrees F," says Cook. "Then, slow and steady is usually best. I'll also use the slow retrieve if water is hot, for example, over 85 degrees F."

His second favorite lure for shallow water is the jig-n-pig. The bass professional usually selects a 1/2-ounce Arkie Flippin' Jig. He will add either a #1 or a #11 Uncle Josh frog when fishing cooler water.

On days when the water and air temperature exceed 75 degrees F, Cook will usually employ a plastic frog such as Ditto's Chunky Frog. According to the Oklahoma pro, this bait will produce a certain amount of vibration on the fall. Again, he'll flip the lure to every piece of cover that he can find.

Ken Cook may opt for a spinnerbait or jig in most shallow waters, but when visibility is minimal, he likes to crank a Big "N".

Resident Bass

"Shallow water fish of this type, i.e., muddy water with good cover, are often 'stay-at-home' fish," says the former fisheries biologist. "They react to adverse weather by getting deeper and tighter into their home cover. Slower and more deliberate retrieves and finesse presentations under these conditions, will usually produce some fish."

A good example was in the 1985 BASS Classic on the Arkansas River in Pine Bluff. Cook caught all his fish, placing seventh, on a 1/2 oz. Gold Eagle spinnerbait with a #5 blade. He was fishing in water less than two feet deep and the water temperature was 85 to 90 degrees F.

"There were lots of horizontal logs and vertical stumps in the backwater," Cook explains. "In cloudy times, the bass were 'loose', but in sunny weather they were more predictable by being under the shade of a horizontal log. I retrieved the bait parallel to each log very slowly and the fish were available."

It was very important to make a perfect cast on the first try. The fish seemed to be spooked by a cast perpendicular to the log. Every one of Cook's fish came on the first cast alongside a log.

The Cover Difference

George Cochran, of North Little Rock, Arkansas is very familiar with the area of river that Cook talks about and with the event, having participated in both Classics held there. He agrees with Cook and other professional anglers that boat position and lure presentation to the fish are the most important aspects to successfully fishing shallow water.

Cochran, like Cook, likes to fish spinnerbaits in most shallow water situations. The amount of cover that he is fishing is also extremely important to the Arkansas pro.

"If you are fishing shallow water that has a lot of cover, the fish will not be easily spooked and you can get closer and fish more effectively," Cochran says, "But if the shallow water does not have a lot of cover, the fish will be more spooky and harder to catch."

He, along with the other professionals, knows what to look for when after shallow water bass. The water types where thin water can be found not only vary from marshes and swamps, ponds and potholes, to large impoundments and small pits, but each offers different parameters that 'dictate' an optimal technique.

These professionals have their own ways to analyze shallow water systems and become proficient at "harvesting" the bounty. Any angler at any level of expertise can do the same.

CHAPTER 4

MARKEROLOGY

Locating And Relocating Techniques

LOCATING FISH. That's the most important aspect to fishing. Most people can catch them once they are near a concentration. But that is not the hard part.

Finding bass is the first part of the picture; marking their location in order to make the most effective presentation is a component of successfully fishing a school of bass. Another part of the picture, if you are going to return the following day, is re-locating the great spot.

To a structure fisherman, the use of marker buoys or natural markers is often a must. Knowing how to use both is what often separates the professional anglers from the novices. How they go about placing marker buoys and establishing the exact location of a bass concentration should be enlightening.

Tennessee bass pro, Charlie Ingram, uses marker buoys in areas where he feels there are going to be fish, as well as where he has caught fish. The professional angler used a unique marker during a tournament one time in Eufala, Alabama. He was fishing river ledges and catching bass.

Doctor's Cure

"I took an aspirin bottle with a 1/2 ounce slip sinker and tied it on 10 lb test line," says Ingram. "Every time I'd catch one fish, I could cast back in there and catch 8 or 10 from the same area. They were so bunched up," he recalls. "I'd back up about 20 yards and drop the aspirin bottle out. Then I'd position my boat on the bottle and throw to where I knew the fish were concentrated."

"I had five spots on a two-mile section of the river, and I just made a complete circle out of those spots all day," explains Ingram. "I caught 44 pounds, 10 ounces in two days off those marker buoys."

Those markers were not very obvious to other fishermen. You can't see an aspirin bottle very easily, and they were undoubtedly more effective during that competition than bright-colored marker buoys.

If Ingram is fishing a ledge and catches a fish on it, he'll immediately throw a buoy out simply to mark the place where he caught that fish. He'll then concentrate on fishing that area. He may leave it

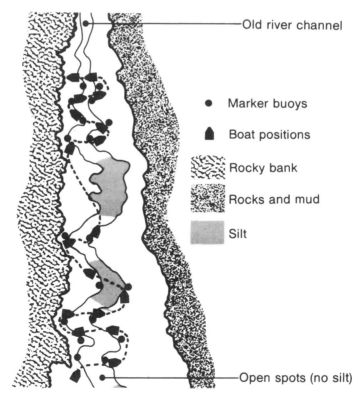

FIGURE 4—*Search for submerged channel areas with your depth finder and mark the creek with buoys, once you have located potentially-productive habitat.*

for a while, but he will come back to it. Normally, when a fish is found on the ledge, it's not there by itself.

"If you find a point on a ledge, you can drop a marker and come back 20 minutes later and fish it much more effectively," he says. "I'll normally drop the marker where the boat should be positioned so I can fish the key spot more effectively and not have to worry about a fish getting tangled up in the line. I'll visually line up with something on the bank or the other side of the point that I'm casting to."

Natural Landmarks

One of Ingram's favorite natural markers is a gap in the trees. He uses that type of natural marker a lot at night on Tennessee's Lake Pickwick. Over the years, he has located some ledges in the middle of the lake, and he'll easily line up on them by using the gaps along the treeline.

"If you find fish on a ledge and want to go back to them the next day, just a small, inconspicuous marker is best," he notes. "If you know the general vicinity, you can pull right up to it," explains Ingram. "You'll generally use a shoreline mark to get you in the general area and then find the smaller object that has been placed there."

Tommy Martin prefers to use natural markers when he can. When fishing deep water, 20 to 25 feet, with a lot of standing timber like that found on Toledo Bend, Sam Rayburn, or even Rodman Pool in Florida, you can use trees or stumps for markers, according to the bass professional.

"You can relate your distance from them when you catch a fish or locate a school of fish," he points out. "I use my depth finder to determine depth of water and then I refer to the stump to determine my position. I can then mark my position without having to put a marker buoy out."

Martin likes to use something on the shoreline, like a clump of grass or root system, as a reference point. He'll frequently do this on a shallow water shoreline that looks much the same. If the area has

Professional anglers frequently use markers, both natural and buoys, to locate bass-holding structures beneath the surface. Use of such is vital to success on waters that have little in the way of distinct visual patterns.

two or three miles of shoreline and he catches three or four fish in practice on a short stretch, he'll look for some type of marker on that shoreline so that he can return to it during the tournament.

"You have to make mental notes of these things to get back to the exact areas," cautions Martin. "If you don't pay attention to the shoreline or mark the spot, you'll find yourself unsure that you are back on the spot where you caught the fish."

Open Water Reference

"I can recall many instances when I was on a lake two or three miles from shore fishing in open water; the depth was pretty much the same, and there were no reference points," he says. "There's really no way to mark the location by water depth, so what I'll do is use marker buoys, which I'd later pick up and move."

Martin has done that often where he has found schools out in open water and just needed a reference point. When he won a major tournament on Sam Rayburn, one of the things he credited was the use of buoys. He was catching bass in deep hydrilla in about 20 feet of water.

"Every morning, when I would first catch a fish, I'd drop a marker buoy immediately," says Martin. "I'd be fighting the bass with one hand and tossing out the marker buoy with the other, to the other side of the boat, not on top of where I caught the fish. I was expecting there would be more fish on that spot."

The buoy would still be unwinding as he was bringing up the fish and netting it. Martin would then back off the marker buoy and start circling around the spot. The professional was very persistent and worked the area thoroughly. Without a reference point, you can lose your location very quickly in open water and not catch as many fish.

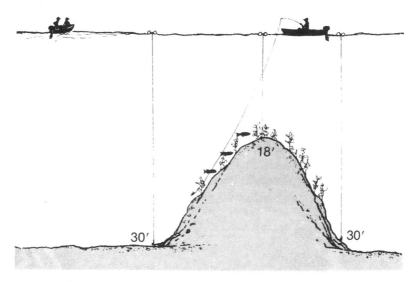

FIGURE 5—*If you are fishing bass located on the side of a hump, then drop the marker buoys as shown, one on top of the high point and two at its base.*

To Denny Brauer, natural markers usually mean a tree or tree line out in the lake that he can line up on to find another hidden spot. Shoreline markers can be docks, trees, homes, a number of things, but the professional angler from Camdenton, Missouri, makes sure that whatever he uses to line up with, that it is permanent.

Documentation

On hard-to-find spots, he believes it's a good idea to have backup markers, just in case something changes. Brauer advises writing these down, and not simply trusting them to memory.

"No matter what you use, try to triangulate the spot to make it easy and precise to find," says Brauer. "In rivers, the channel buoy markers can be great to line up on, but be aware that they can change from season to season."

"Try to find areas out of the main natural flow of boat traffic and you have already disguised yourself, the fish, and the spot you're fishing from 75 percent of the other fishermen," advises Brauer. "I've marked some brush piles and grass beds with small pieces of styrofoam and cork tied to a length of monofilament," he says. "These are tough for passing boats to spot and can save you time."

Disguised Markers

Tommy Martin also uses disguised markers on occasion, such as when he finds a school of fish in open water during practice. To get back to that spot when the competition starts, he takes several approaches. Sometimes, he'll take a little stick that would not look unusual floating around in the water and tie a light piece of monofilament, six or eight pound test, to it. A big sinker will make that marker complete.

Martin, like Brauer, will also mark a precise spot by using very small pieces of styrofoam. Once he knows exactly how deep the water is, he'll adjust the length of line so that the heavy weight pulls the styrofoam down three or four inches below the surface of the water.

When an angler is far from any definitive shore point, marker buoys will add fish to the stringer. They should be placed near the bass concentration but not on top of them to minimize the chances of a hooked fish fouling the marker line.

To find a general area two or three miles offshore, some type of reference point on the bank is needed to line up with. Martin tries to triangulate several points on shore to find the general vicinity so that he can locate his submerged styrofoam markers. Once he gets back in that area, the professional bass angler will ease around with his trolling motor until he pinpoints the exact spot. That marking system has been very popular among tournament fishermen.

Martin used the disguised marker system on Lake Okeechobee in a major tournament. He was fishing an area on the extreme north end of Okeechobee when he ran up on a little four foot shoal. Bass were breaking everywhere, feeding on shad. Although it was only 8:30 a.m., he and his partner already had limits of May bass.

They stopped the outboard and used their electric motor to troll up to them. The two anglers started catching bass immediately, but the fish were not really large enough to cull with. They had fish of the same size in their livewells that they had caught on another small shoal.

47

Martin wanted to mark the spot, because he figured that the bass would reappear there at the same time the next morning. He pulled his little disguised markers out of his rod box and positioned one properly. The next day, he had to spend about 30 minutes locating his marker.

The 45-year old bass pro finally got on the right spot and caught a couple of keepers. The fish never did come up and break like they did the day before, but the spot did produce two fish that day that Martin needed badly. Marking such a spot can be very important in any kind of fishing.

The difference between a nice catch and a single fish or two is often determined by an angler's ability to locate a concentration. As these seasoned professionals know, correctly marking the 'find' is vital to future success.

CHAPTER 5

BOAT POSITIONING

Boat Control—Keys To Success

A MOST CRITICAL part of fishing is boat positioning, according to professional angler, Denny Brauer. He has seen new boat owners make a big mistake by not understanding the importance of boat control.

"I notice them running into boat docks on Lake of the Ozarks all the time," says Brauer. "Anytime you bump the cover, especially with shallow fish, you will spook them."

"Everyone relates boat control primarily to flippin'," he points out. "Granted, boat control is very critical to certain techniques, but it's critical to any technique, even if you are working deep cover. Many times I'm vertical-jigging a spoon and the lure position has to be very precise."

"Whether it's foot or hand-controlled, when you touch that button, you have to be aware in what direction the trolling motor will move the boat," Brauer advises. "After a while, running it will be as easy as walking. You aren't even thinking about doing it, and that's the way it has to be to correctly control the boat."

The biggest problem may be getting in a hurry once in a while, according to the tournament angler and guide. Trolling motors are often ran at too high a speed. Anglers come in on the cover too fast and end up reversing the direction. Then, they're blowing pressure waves back at the fish while trying to stop the forward momentum of the boat.

Brauer believes that doing such will automatically handicap the angler and keep him from catching at least the larger fish. While the smaller fish are not affected, the bigger fish are extremely sensitive to that type of commotion. Your approach must be quieter.

Denny Brauer's vast experience with boats has allowed him to be more successful on the professional tournament trail.

Control Operations

"I like to work into the wind so that, when I do catch a fish and get off the trolling motor, I won't drift into the school," he points out. "I'll drift away from them. That allows me to control everything. I won't drift in on the fish too fast because the wind is not controlling me."

Brauer will use every speed on his trolling motor, depending on the cover, its density and the patterns that are effective. He may run on high 24-volt all day long; other days he'll set the speed extremely slow on 12-volt. When he is working very shallow water in a small area with a slow-type bait like a jig or worm, Brauer may be on "low 24."

One thing that he doesn't like to do is turn the trolling motor on and off a lot. Brauer prefers to find a speed that is consistent with the cover so that it can be worked thoroughly.

"I like to slowly move along an area and keep running the motor right on through, rather than stop and go, stop and go," explains Brauer. "I think the stop and go can be a turnoff for fish. I wish that I could be underwater at times to see if they relate to the sounds and vibration of the on and off switch."

To effectively fish any area, the key factors are selecting the right speed and how you approach the cover. Brauer runs on higher trolling motor speeds in tournament practice than he ever would during the actual event. He is trying to cover as much water as possible then and not trying to catch a bunch of fish. He wants only to look at a lot of cover and draw a few strikes to determine the active areas.

"During practice, I'm often not sure how I will do in a tournament because I prefer to cover water quickly," says Brauer. "I don't want to slow down to work it thoroughly because I may not be able to find any fish at all."

Fighting Control

Another important consideration in boat control comes into play when the bass has struck the bait. You have to be very aware of where the fish is in relation to the trolling motor. If the fish makes a run toward the shaft, you may need to maneuver your rod to prevent an entanglement.

On some occasions when Brauer hooks a big fish in open water, he reachs down and lifts the electric from the water. He'll then trim up the big engine by pushing down on the bow-mounted switch with his toe.

"While you are doing that, you can control the fish with the rod," he explains, "as long as he's moving away from you."

Brauer feels that the location of the trolling motor is a matter of individual preference. He's left handed and mounts his on the right side. The six-foot two-inch tall professional likes the fact that he can make a cast and put the trolling motor down at the same time, or fight a big fish while pulling the motor up, if needed.

This is most advantageous for tournament fishermen, where every cast and every fish counts. The placement and handling of the trolling motor may make a difference of only 50 casts over a day, but that could mean the difference between going to a major year-end tournament event or not.

Brauer lived in Nebraska for several years and often fished a pond with a favorite stump out in a mud flat, from which he could always catch a bass. One day, he worked the area all around the stump and nothing struck his bait.

"I got in too close to it," recalls Brauer. "I had the trolling motor turned around and you could actually see silt blowing out underneath the stump. I just happened to drop my bait down beside it. With all the water churning, a four pounder grabbed the bait on its retrieve out. That fish couldn't have been two foot from the head of

The angler should be cognizant of the trolling motor at all times, especially when fishing areas of heavy cover. Brauer prefers to battle a fish up close on his terms.

the trolling motor when he grabbed that lure. The semi-stained water was blowing right into his face."

Like many, Brauer believes that the more often fish are pressured, the more accustomed they get to trolling motor sounds. Fish that are accustomed to the sounds probably aren't scared but are put on alert, according to the Evinrude-sponsored pro. At other times, the bass may not even know what the trolling motor noise is. It varies from water to water.

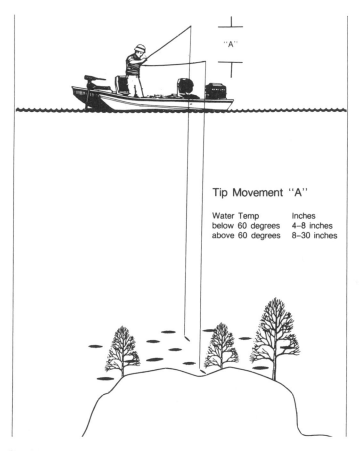

Tip Movement "A"

Water Temp	Inches
below 60 degrees	4–8 inches
above 60 degrees	8–30 inches

FIGURE 6—*The more often fish are pressured, the more accustomed they get to a trolling motor above them. In muddy waters or those with high boat traffic, vertical fishing can be extremely productive.*

Foot Or Hand?

Brauer uses a foot control because he doesn't want any wasted movement. He figures that particular type is best today.

"Many professionals like a hand-operated model and I ran one for a year, but I still think it's a disadvantage," he says. "Motors nowadays are made so you no longer have to worry about the cable breaking. A lot of people began using the hand-controls because they thought that they would hold up better under all conditions."

"I carry an additional trolling motor in my rod locker just for insurance," notes Brauer, "and in three years, I've yet had to use it. That should tell you how well equipment is built these days."

Brauer fishes shallow water a lot and he loves to flip. In such an environment, he feels that a quiet motor is critical. You can't afford to spook fish.

Noise Considerations

"I can remember when my trolling motor would hit the bottom and I would see baitfish scatter across the surface," he points out. "Whenever that happened, you can't tell me that any bass there didn't also get spooked. I don't see that any more with the trolling motor that I'm running now."

"It's not just the sound of the motor. You can't let the bracket get loose so that everytime you hit the bottom it clangs. You can't let the prop get all burred-up and put out additional pressure waves. Those are things that you can control, and you need to be aware of the noise the trolling motor makes."

"There's no quieter electric motor than Evinrude," smiles Brauer. "But, just like any motor, you have to maintain it," he adds. "When I'm on the road for three or four weeks at a time, I always take care of the motor. There may be bolts that need to be tightened or other things that need to be taken care of. When you use the equipment as much as I do, you have to be aware of its condition."

Brauer prefers a trolling motor positioned fairly high in the water. The prop should not break the surface but in shallow water it keeps him from worrying about hitting a stump and bending a shaft.

The author finds boat control critical when fishing fast-moving lures. You don't have time to correct for the boat's momentum if you make a mistake.

"Why have it all the way down if you are fishing in three feet of water," he says. "It's a handicap. When fishing structure in rough water with large waves pushing at you, the prop shouldn't come out of the water every few seconds when the bow of the boat comes up. You can drop the motor back down some then and adapt it to the conditions as they change."

Propulsion Points

Brauer pays careful attention to his trolling motor prop and will quickly change it if conditions warrant. When the vegetation is so heavy that he has to constantly pull up the motor and clean the prop, he'll go to a weedless prop to penetrate the cover.

"Most companies today have a motor designed for a weedless prop that will handle any kind of vegetation, and that's good,"

Brauer stresses, "but in some cases the angler can go back to the regular props when he doesn't need the weedless feature. They are often quieter and probably have a little more thrust."

"When fishing open water or brush where there is no vegetation, I use a non-weedless prop," he explains. "It's up to the angler and his fishing conditions to determine whether or not he needs it. It's nice, though, that we have the option."

You have to be able to get to the honey hole if you're going to fish it. The approach is the key to catching bass once you are there Brauer thinks. His tournament accomplishments certainly reflect how his careful and planned approach works.

To the Missouri pro, the trolling motor is a vital piece of fishing equipment; one that deserves the upmost in attention. Maintenance and operation knowledge are critical to any productive angler.

CHAPTER 6

BACKSEAT STRATEGIES

Success From The Rear Of The Boat

SOMETIMES IT TAKES more than a little luck to catch more fish from the rear casting platform than from the front. In most circles, an angler in front and one in the back is the name of the game.

The person up front generally has first shot at many of the targets that may hold fish. Bass are competitive and react quickly to the presentation. More often than not, they'll strike at the first lure cast to their hiding spot. Consequently, the angler casting from the bow often catches more fish.

That doesn't always have to be the case, though, particularly if the person in the stern area is knowledgeable concerning back-seat strategies. There are ways to maximize the catch from the rear, and most of the touring tournament professionals know a few tricks.

Larry Nixon has fished from the back of many competing fishermen's boats, and the pro usually catches more fish than they do.

"The backseat fisherman cannot be afraid of what the guy in front is doing or afraid of getting behind him," says Nixon. "The backseat fisherman should be real observant of what the fisherman in front is covering and leaving. There's no way the man in the bow can cover all that water unless the man in front is flippin' or working a distinct bank pattern. Then the back seat angler does have a little bit of a problem."

Lure Variations

The backseat angler can fish just as effectively by observing the angler in front and fishing the unused water. If the guy is using a

Larry Nixon has compiled an impressive history of winning tournaments and, of necessity, catching bass. Not all of his bass catching occurs in the bow. He is equally adept at pulling them over the stern.

spinnerbait or topwater lure in front, Nixon believes that you can use a jig or worm behind him and catch just as many fish.

"A lot of it is using a different lure," he explains. "You cannot compete with a man who has a very effective bank technique by using the same lure. But you can, if you use another lure that catches fish at a different level than the lure he's using!"

"In my second year of major bass tournament fishing on Lake Powell in Arizona, Fred Ward, one of the better fishermen out west, was my partner," says Nixon. "Fred was moving through the water fairly fast and would usually leave between 25 to 30 feet between each spot. I would just pinpoint my cast between each of his and I wound up catching seven fish that weighed 21 pounds. His seven fish weighed 17 pounds."

"I was fishing a little slower and letting my bait fall all the way to the bottom," explains Nixon. "Once you have observed where he's fishing and what is left, you must still work the lure properly," he points out. "If you're fishing right, and you've covered the water right, you ought to catch as many bass as the guy in front."

Gary Klein, professional bass angler from Oroville, California, believes that fishing from the back seat can be a great advantage.

"The angler controlling the boat is limited to where he can cast, and that's the forward part of the boat as he positions down a bank," explains Klein. "The angler in the rear has his mind free of boat control and can make more casts, cover more water, and devote more thought to his fishing."

"He has to work hand-in-hand with the guy up front," he adds. "If the guy in front has found a concentration of fish in the area, I would prefer to fish from the back," Klein says. "Once he makes a cast, he's committed to that cast and I can throw anywhere else I want to."

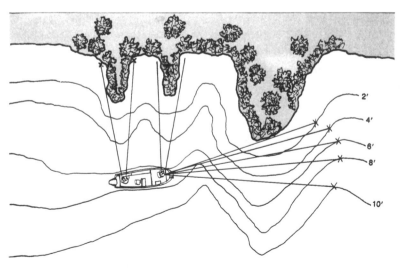

FIGURE 7—*The two anglers in a boat should work together for maximum productivity. The angler in the stern is usually left shots that the man on the bow misses under any conditions.*

Competition Urges

The problem that most anglers have when fishing out of the back, according to Klein, is that they feel they have to compete with the other angler in the boat. "That's not what you're there for," he says, "you're there to figure out the fish and compete against them."

"One of the greatest tournament experiences that I ever had was with Ricky Clunn," says Klein. "I drew him in a Texas event and we were fishing a typical creek that was very narrow, in my boat. Both of us could reach either shoreline," he says. "It was the second day of the tournament and I was in third place with about 20 pounds. Ricky was out of the tournament and only had about three pounds of fish."

"Ricky gave me everything, all the first shots, and never once threw in front of me or to the bank on the other side," says Klein. "He knew that I was going to go up one side and down the other. I was slow-rolling a spinnerbait right by targets and brushing the blade against them to catch quality bass," he explains. "Ricky sat on top of my outboard and proceeded to 'lace' me. He was catching three to every one of mine and had a quick limit."

"The reason he was able to do this is that he wasn't even thinking about me," says Klein. "He wasn't trying to throw the spinnerbait on the same targets that I was. He developed a pattern in my area and that pattern was on shade. I was fishing by the fish and he was sitting in the back catching them."

"If any other angler would have gotten into my boat to compete with me on my targets, they wouldn't have caught but one or two fish. I still would have gotten my limit. But here was someone on my back seat with a whole different approach."

Weather Problems

"Naturally, in bad weather the guy up front is fighting the trolling motor. I had several occurrences on the tournament circuit where I have actually let my partners run the trolling motor," he says. "In bad weather, they'll be busy trying to get the first shot and fighting with the trolling motor."

Most of the top professionals in the country have fished from the rear of the boat. They have developed strategies that work there on bass.

"The second day of a Lake Gaston bass tournament, my partner ran to the bow of my boat first thing," says Klein. "I didn't say anything. I decided to concentrate on the fish and had five strikes that day," he says. "They weighed 21 pounds on the scales and my partner never caught the first fish."

"He was over-fishing the area," explains Klein. "He should have slowed down and thought about the fish rather than about what I was doing."

Randy Fite, who has fished several tournaments on timber-strewn Toledo Bend, agrees that when the wind blows on a lake like that, you can be fighting the timber and trolling motor more than you are fishing.

"The person in the back is fishing all day long with plenty of targets," says Fite. "There is no advantage in being at the front of the boat in those conditions; it's a big advantage being in the back of the boat."

"If I am just weekend fishing or the targets are not that specific, I'll stand in the back and closely watch the person in front," says the Texas pro. "I'll try to fish the area utilizing both our efforts. It's not a wise decision to be doing exactly the same thing as the person in front."

"If he's fishing isolated targets, he may be catching most of the fish, but there should be other fish in the area using a different pattern, or they may be out a little deeper," says Fite. "Therefore, I'll change my fishing to something different than the person in the front is doing and try to catch totally different fish than the ones he's after. That strategy has worked well for me in the past."

Fite believes that it can be a tremendous advantage being in the back, not having to worry about the trolling motor in high winds or in stumpy areas. You can totally concentrate on the fishing.

Bow Watch

Bass professional Harold Allen has been a guide and touring tournament angler for more than ten years. In that period, he's seen the back of the boat several times and has been very successful at catching fish. Allen has learned to watch the angler in the bow closely.

"The first thing you have to do is to key in on his style of operating the boat," Allen says. "You should notice how he stays off a bank or runs into one when fishing. In what manner does he run a boat? In doing that," he adds, "you have to fish defensively and offensively both at the same time."

"Once I figure out how a guy operates a boat, then I can start trying to figure out how I can work the water that I have available to me," explains Allen. "I'll try to determine if what he's throwing is effectively covering what is there. Whether he's catching fish or not is very obvious."

"I'll often throw a different bait to cover the water, a different type but not necessarily a different color of lure," he says. "A different presentation may work."

62

In a Gaston, Virginia tournament, Allen had found some fish under boat docks but unfortunately, the wind was really blowing in on them. The water depth and visibility were good and the fish were holding there.

"While fighting the trolling motor to hold the boat where I could cast properly to the docks, I was messing up my casts," comments Allen. "I was getting about one cast out of three where I wanted it. Jerry Rhynn was fishing out of the back of my boat, not worrying about the operation of the trolling motor," he notes. "He caught several bass that day!"

Knowing the 'productive' way to fish from the back of a boat, whether its a car topper or 20-foot bass boat, will enhance your catch.

"In high winds, the guy in the back can more effectively fish deep water," Allen notes. "I fished the 1985 U.S. Open in Las Vegas and I started out in the back because that's where I wanted to be," he explains. "The water was deep and the winds were high. I wanted to concentrate on the fishing."

"My partner would just forget about the trolling motor once he pulled up on the structure, though. We would be fishing 20 feet of water one minute and 30 seconds later, we'd be fishing 50. After 10 minutes I got up front and ran the trolling motor," laughs Allen. "That's why it's so important to watch the guy in front when you first get in the boat to see how he operates it. Then, you can get your own game plan going."

The next time you are in the back of the boat, these pros caution you not to despair. Some of the best fishing can be had, if you have a strategy.

CHAPTER 7

WATER pH CHANGES

Monitoring Concepts For Locating Bass

I HAD NO IDEA what my pH Monitor was doing to reveal the readings that were supposed to help me catch more bass. It was my first on-the-water experimentation with the unit, and I didn't really care how it arrived at the numbers. I was pragmatic. I just wanted to see the thing work.

The concept of utilizing pH levels to help anglers locate fish was developed by University of Oklahoma zoologist, Dr. Loren Hill, in the 70's. His studies of the relationship between water quality and bass behavior was the basis for a Lakes Systems unit that monitors pH readings to find "optimal" levels.

That's what I was looking for, optimal levels, on my first trip several years ago on a phosphate pit, but I never did find them. The results of the experimentation, however, were impressive. I caught seven bass in about an hour while fishing water with pH values closest to the "optimal" levels.

Several trips since have confirmed my confidence in locating the pH values closest to the ideal range for maximum bass action. Today, my favorite tool is the Multi-C-Lector, which reveals the whole spectrum of water chemistry characteristics. Many other anglers have also used these tools, including some of the nation's top professionals.

"Sometimes, simply understanding the 'why' of things makes it easier to gain confidence in your decisions," says biologist-turned-professional angler, Ken Cook. "Knowing just how pH works explains why bass will seek certain coves for spawning."

"Coves with pH ranging 7.5 to 7.9, or closest to it, allow most successful reproduction for largemouth bass," he explains. "I use this information in the spring to locate coves that have the most active spawning bass."

Cook is one of the most successful tournament anglers ever to grip a fishing rod. The Meers, Oklahoma resident has had at least half a dozen impressive victories in major events held around the country. Formerly with the Oklahoma Department of Wildlife Conservation, his life changed dramatically with a $100,000 victory on the St. Johns River. He decided to go into the professional ranks on a full-time basis. His success since has made him happy with that decision.

Biological Edge

You might think that a pro angler with a fish biology background would have an edge on other competitors. That knowledge does help him. One of the keys to his ability in finding bass on a large body of water is knowing the water quality/bass relationship. To Ken Cook, the pH value is significant year around.

"In summer, pH breaklines become the most important location depth for bass," says the professional. "I use this depth location information to determine how deep to fish. Knowledge about other things that affect pH, such as photosynthesis, helps me to quickly adjust during the fishing day to keep up after bass movements," says Cook.

"For instance, at Lake Granbury during a major bass tournament, the pH breakline was three to five feet deep in early morning," he explains. "I could catch bass with topwater baits until about 10 a.m. That's when the pH increased."

"The stronger mid-day sun forced an increase in the photosynthesis rate, which caused the pH to climb at the surface," says Cook. "That made the bass stay deeper in the breakline and move away from shore. They were less active because the increased pH was less conducive to activity," he explains, "and thus, the bass were much more difficult to catch!"

"At that time, I moved up lake where the water was muddier," says the professional. "The photosynthesis rate wasn't affected as much at two to three foot depths," he continued. "The bass there were somewhat more active."

To professional bass angler Ken Cook, pH readings mean a lot. The former fisheries biologist utilizes the information to help him find more largemouth.

Cook started out in the middle of the lake and watched the good spots get inundated with boats. Places like outer bends with flooded trees were so popular that as soon as one boat would leave, another would show up and replace it.

He won the tournament, not by joining the crowds, but by fishing places where the locals and touring pros weren't. He would move away from a channel to less-than-desirable habitat, for example, where there weren't a lot of bass, but enough. The Granbury fish were more catchable there than in the good cover receiving heavy pressure.

Summer Patterns

"I use the meter to locate the pH breakline in the summer when the water temperatures exceed the mid-sixties," explains Cook. "By lowering the probe at one foot intervals, I can locate the depth at which the pH changes rapidly. That information tells me where to find the most active fish."

"Why this is, we don't know yet," he adds. "But it sure works."

"I then use that depth contour to locate either suspended fish, or better yet, fish that are in cover at that depth," says Cook. "If you have active fish in structure, then those will be catchable fish."

"The pH is affected by several things, including rain water," he says. "Muddy water is caused by runoff rainfall, which is low pH. When this meets the clear water which is usually higher pH, you have in effect a vertical pH breakline. That's why active fish are found where clear and muddy water meet."

"Rainfall runoff can also help in the spring, when largemouth bass require pH of 7.5 to 7.9 to spawn successfully," says Cook. "The runoff causes lower pH. That, in turn, can cause isolated areas to provide suitable pH for reproductive success if the lake water is higher pH."

"That helps in two ways," he explains. "First of all, it concentrates spawning bass in these areas of proper pH, and secondly, if this is a recurring situation it can lead to areas with good annual reproduction of bass. The body of water would, thus, have a good bass population."

Plant Considerations

"In the summer, pH is affected greatly by the photosynthesis of green plants, such as hydrilla and phytoplankton," says Cook. "The phytoplankton produces most of the oxygen in the water by photosynthesis and thereby produces the most change in pH. That's because the sheer mass of those plants is most fertile."

The quantity of plants and its effect on pH is controlled by the water's fertility, according to Cook. Water that is green from plant life will have a great variation in pH during the day. Also, areas with lots of moss, such as hydrilla or milfoil, will have significant pH changes. This often causes fishing to be excellent around moss beds in the early morning and to quickly deteriorate after the sun comes up.

Plant photosynthesis and rain runoff cause changes in the pH of shallow waters. The author monitors water chemistry with the aid of a Multi-C-Lector. That leads to better fishing.

"We've always thought that this was because of the sun directly," he points out, "but more likely it's because of the sun's effect on the rate of photosynthesis in the plants present."

"A good example of this happened at a U.S. Bass Invitational on Sam Rayburn Lake," he says. "I could catch several fish each morning with topwater baits around some hydrilla beds. By 9 a.m., though, with bright sun, the bass retreated into much deeper water. The pH reading was 8.2 at 9 a.m. and up to 9.5 by 10 a.m."

"The bass moved back under the protection of the overhead weed beds," says Cook. "Photosynthesis there was negligible and there was no mixing of the layers to alleviate the situation."

Not even Ken Cook catches bass everytime out, but you don't have to be a professional angler or a fisheries biologist to apply certain pH concepts which should help you catch more fish.

CHAPTER 8

WATER COLOR CHANGES

Utilizing Visibility Limitations

MUDDY WATER PROBLEMS certainly don't have to be. The successful anglers use this environmental parameter to their advantage, and they often catch several bass. Cooperative largemouth can be found in waters of any visibility.

Heavy rains and winds can cause water to quickly muddy. Wave action occurs where boating activity or strong winds are prevalent. The waves breaking against a dirt bank or across a silted bar will usually stain the waters in close proximity. Those same waves knock baitfish and other forage around and that means the dinner bell has rung for the largemouth. Disoriented prey is easy to catch. Bass quickly learn the advantage they have in foraging during wind and wave action.

Muddy waters caused from wave disturbance often have a distinct edge. Bass may hold on the clear-water edge of a mudline and wait for the hapless forage, or they may move into the dirty water. If they hold in the clearer stuff, they'll not have problems in sighting their food, or a forage-resembling lure that passes.

While some anglers are apprehensive when it comes to tossing a bait into muddy water, those anglers who have discovered how to systematically and effectively work such are avid dirty water searchers. The condition helps them find fish. To professional tournament anglers, guides, and even outdoor writers, that's important. Even to the weekend "pro", the productive techniques of dealing with waters of low visibility should be of extreme interest.

"Most fish found in muddy water are relatively shallow, between six inches to four feet deep," says bass pro Charlie Ingram. "Fish feel more secure with less light penetration in the water, and are usually shallower," he explains. "Generally, that's where the baitfish are to be found."

"Water will muddy up after a rain, and the fish will be in the runoff where the water will be cooler and have more oxygen," he points out.

First Clear Area

"In a muddy water situation, I look for the first area that's starting to clear," Ingram says. "I sometimes find a clear water section five feet out from a bank. Most of the time, the baitfish will move to that clear water area on the bank. If you can find that type situation with the baitfish in it, the bass will be there."

In the cooler months, Ingram likes to fish the clearer water around the banks with a jig. In a runoff, he'll use a spinnerbait or crankbait. Normally he will select a larger gold-colored blade because he feels that it's more attractive to the fish.

In muddy water, though, Ingram will normally use a white skirt or, if it's extremely muddy, a chartreuse and orange skirt on the spinnerbait. He's found that fish caught out of muddy water are usually very pale in color. The baitfish there should be also, and he uses a similar color skirt on the spinnerbait.

"I use a dark-colored jig because I feel it's more highly visible to bass," Ingram adds. "I like a black with a little chartreuse in it, or

FIGURE 8—*Muddy, runoff waters contain food items, such as small organisms which attract baitfish, and in turn, bass. Dark waters also tend to hold more heat and consequently offer more active bass.*

something to give it a little contrast. In clear water, I'll use a blue jig."

In a muddy water situation, the professional selects a crankbait with an orange belly. He has found that an all red crankbait is very good in muddy water situations where there is a long, shallow flat dropping off into a creek channel.

"This lure used over any shallow water dropoff is productive," says Ingram. "I like to use a vibrating bait with a rattle in it that makes some kind of noise."

The Spook Factor

Ingram finds fish easier to catch in muddy water because they're not as spooky. He can usually get the boat right on top of them and they won't be aware of his presence. The most important thing he looks for in a muddy water situation is that first clearing water, whether it be in the back of the creek, in a runoff or around the bank somewhere.

"If the water temperature is below 80 degrees, I'll fish it with a jig or spinnerbait," he advises. "In warmer water, I'll use a spinnerbait or crankbait."

If asked to make a choice for most occasions, he'll have an answer as most pros do. Overall, Ingram relies on a spinnerbait in muddy water because it gives off a flash from the sunlight. It can be fished slowly, so the fish can catch it easily.

Waters of low visibility have confronted Rick Clunn throughout his career in professional fishing. The angler is well known for his successes in dirty water.

Shallow Basics

Muddy water fishing is fairly basic except in extreme cold water conditions, according to Clunn. He has observed that muddy water has the universal effect of allowing the fish to be very shallow and usually right against the bank or a shallow object. Those are favorable conditions for the angler.

Muddy water doesn't have to pose insurmountable problems to anglers. Knowing what baits to toss and how to present the lures is the key to success after the rains.

In extremely muddy water (one to two-inch visibility), Clunn finds the fish that are caught will usually be less than a foot deep. Any bass that are deeper than that are usually not aggressive. The real key to this situation, he believes, is not to work the baits under the fish. Just try to keep the bait on the bank or right against the object (log, stump, etc).

"I tend to slow down my presentation," says Clunn. "The senses that the bass utilizes most under these conditions are one, vibration, which is the most important, and two, sound."

Clunn prefers spinnerbaits that have a high level of vibration even at slow speeds. A current favorite of his is the Stanley Vibra Shaft, a tapered wire spinnerbait. The Texan also likes to use crankbaits that have a wide wobble at slow speeds, fat worms and lizards, and heavy 9/16-ounce jigs. All those lures displace more water and make them easier for the fish to find.

"When working logs that may be in deeper water, swim your baits no deeper than a foot under the log," says Clunn. "In extremely cold water, flipping a jig in very shallow water is about the only technique that might produce," he says. "Fish extremely slow and keep the presentation right on the fish's nose. Even then, he may not bite."

Visibility Stratification

Under certain environmental conditions, the water clarity may change with depth. The water may be relatively clear from the surface down to 10 feet, and then becomes stained at depths greater than

Muddy water considerations are many. Sound and vibration are important parameters in waters of low visibility but color considerations are still significant when making a lure choice.

10 feet. The reason for this phenomenon is that rivers and streams that drain into lakes often carry sediments. This is especially true in the spring, or after periods of much rainfall.

According to Dr. Loren Hill, developer of the Color-C-Lector, the water is more dense because of the suspended sediments. The stained water will settle across the bottom or deeper sections of lakes. For those who own a Color-C-Lector or Multi-C-Lector, the situation can be detected by a sudden drop of the instrument's reading as a result of the lack of light penetration.

"When this phenomenon is detected at a depth the fish are holding, read the next lower color band," says Hill. "If the probe is lowered slowly into the water and you don't lose sight of it within the first four feet, you will be reading the 'clear' color band scale. Then if the needle jumps as the probe is lowered through the 10 foot depth, you would want to go to the 'stained' water band."

Water clarity is significantly related to a fish's ability to see colors, according to Dr. Hill. The key to using his Color-C-Lector in waters of varying visibilities is determining which of the three major color bands (clear, stained, or muddy) to read. And that's fairly easy in most waters.

Regardless of the ways you go about finding bass, the fact remains that understanding muddy waters influence on bass behavior will help an angler put more fish in the boat. Muddy waters occur sooner or later, and the angler who knows how to handle the mild alteration will succeed.

CHAPTER 9

WATER LEVEL CHANGES

Effects Of Elevation Variations

"A SUDDEN DRAWDOWN, forcing the lake's water level to drop rapidly, will cause the bass to back off into deeper water," says Tommy Martin. "A drop of six inches within a week has a significant bearing on the location of the fish. This is especially true in the spring when the bass are first moving up to spawn."

"In the east Texas lakes, like Toledo Bend and Sam Rayburn, hydrilla can be found in six to 15-foot depths during the spring," explains Martin. "We often have a seven or eight-inch drop during the week, and that will move the bass. They will back out of the bushes and into the deeper hydrilla to spawn."

Martin marks the water level of any lake that he is going to fish for several days, or that he is planning on returning to within a few weeks or so. He'll take a small piece of cord or string and wrap it around tree at the water level. He can then return to the same tree and note what change has taken place.

Knowing the level fluctuation during the off-limits period of a tournament may possibly provide information on the whereabouts of bass located in pre-practice. He'll always mark the lake's level during pre-practice and return two or three weeks later for the tournament.

The Corps of Engineers, or other responsible water management authority, also can be consulted for lake level information. When he is unable to pre-practice on a lake, Martin will call them a month before an event and record the reading and date. He will then call them the day before the official practice starts and evaluate the difference.

"They'll generally tell you if they are going to be generating power and dropping the lake, or whether they are going to hold the lake level steady," Martin says. "They're pretty good about telling you what you want to know. You can get that information easily to know if you have to adjust to a rapid drop."

Edge Movements

Fish that were up in the shallow bushes will just drop off into the creeks next to 10 to 13-foot of water. Most of the reservoirs, even those without submerged vegetation like hydrilla, have well-defined creek channels within the coves where the water may drop from five to 15 feet. The bass sense that the water is falling and they stay close to the edges of the channels.

When the lake starts falling, the shad react similarly to the bass by moving out of the very shallow water to the deeper water. On most of the east Texas lakes in the fall, the big schools of threadfin will stay in 30 or 40 feet of water once the level begins to drop. A calm lake in the fall will probably show signs of many shad schools on the surface just before dusk.

When the lake is falling, Martin searches for more vertical banks where the lake bottom quickly drops into the depths.

"On the east Texas lakes, we really don't fish right up on the banks that much," he explains. "We'll fish back in the bushes that are near the bank, the flooded willows and the flooded buck bushes, places like that. Still, the majority of the fish are caught in the outer bushes, the ones farthest out in the lake, because they are near deeper water."

"The bigger bass are usually out there, even in the spring," says Martin. "The big ones won't go way back into the shallow bushes in one or two foot of water. They'll stay out in three to five foot of water next to 10 or 15 foot of water. That's where they'll spawn."

Post-Spawn Effects

In the post-spawn period, when the majority of the bass have finished bedding, a falling lake will have less effect on the fish. A

Tommy Martin derives success on many lakes by analyzing the water level fluctuations. Knowing how such changes affect bass movement is a key to fishing productivity.

rapid drop may still move some fish, though. In the summer, for example, the hydrilla can be found growing in 23 feet of water on Sam Rayburn, and on a big elevation change, the shallow bass may move into it.

If the waters only fall six inches or so over a three-week period, most bass will not be affected, according to the man who has won more than one dozen national bass tournaments. Largemouth on the extremely flat banks would most probably be the exception.

Even in very shallow water, bass on the steeper banks will be less affected by a drop during the post-spawn period. Bushes in four to six foot of water with deep water running up to the bank are favorite spots to fish in the spring when the water is falling, according to Martin.

"A lot of bass will move to their summer pattern as the water temperature rises above 75 degrees. Out in the deep hydrilla, those fish generally won't be affected too much by a falling lake," Martin adds. "During the early part of the summer, they'll move out to the drops on the deep grasslines where the creek channels cut through the grass. When they move to the outer ridges in 15 to 20 foot depths with grass and 30 foot of water all around them, those fish are not affected."

Lakes generally drop the most during the late summer and fall, according to Martin. Rainfall is minimal and the power generation at each dam takes its toll on the water supply in many lakes. Water evaporation, electricity use and irrigation all have an effect on water levels then.

FIGURE 9—*Moving water over a flat can turn on largemouth or, if the level is falling fast, can move them great distances. Bass on flat banks after the spawn will move to deeper, isolated structure that is similar to what is found along the shore.*

Falling Fall

"In the east Texas lakes, we usually see a rapid drop in elevation during August, September and October," says Martin. "Then we go to the deep hydrilla lines out on the ridges in the middle of the lake. A hydrilla bed that is 15 to 18 foot on the edge and drops off into 20 and 30 foot is what we look for."

The fish on the flat lakes in east Texas seldom relate to the banks in the fall, according to Martin. They stay out in the deeper water on the vegetation. Spinnerbaits fished over the grass in seven or eight feet of water are effective on the relatively shallow bass then. The best procedure, though, is fishing heavy baits down on the deeper grass.

On lakes without milfoil or hydrilla, the bass will relate to the banks during the fall. Bass will inhabit the shoreline cover, such as

Reservoir waters can fall quickly when power or irrigation needs demands are high. Water marks on the timber can normally reveal a falling water level.

81

stumps, rocks, etc. When the water is dropping, though, most will be near the steeper banks rather than the flat banks.

Martin fishes a lot of lakes in the fall, when a quick drop in water may push bass off the creek channel banks. His most memorable experience occurred on Joe Wheeler Reservoir in northern Alabama. He won the 1974 Bass Masters Classic under conditions that left most contenders 'hi and dry'.

"It was late October and the lake was falling rapidly," recounts Martin. "We had been told that the waters had been falling for quite some time and that the fish weren't hitting."

When he found out that the reservoir had been dropping so quickly, he established his game plan. On the first day of practice, he fished stumps and bushes in shallow, flat water for three hours. His catch of skinny, 12 and 13-inch bass from the two to three-foot water helped eliminate those type areas.

Steep Channel Drops

Martin then moved out to steeper, vertical banks where creek channels with 10 to 15 feet of water were in close proximity. Large chunk rock and isolated stumps made the place ideal. He started catching two to four pound bass from the cover.

Looking for channel banks became a priority then. Martin fished more vertical, steeper banks with channels nearby, while most of the other fishermen were fishing visible cover out on the flats in very shallow water. The latter were catching only little fish.

Deep, winter fish don't even know the lake is falling, Martin surmises. Bass in 35 or 40 feet of water are not affected at all then. They are not going anywhere, according to the guide.

On most flatland lakes, the water level isn't drawn down rapidly enough to create a current. Mountain lakes in Alabama, Georgia, and Virginia, however, do experience a visible movement of water. Fishing a current requires an adjustment in strategy also.

"I was tossing a worm on Lake Moultrie in South Carolina near where the canal comes into the lake," relates Martin. "The water was really flowing, and I was fishing a sandbar with some difficulty.

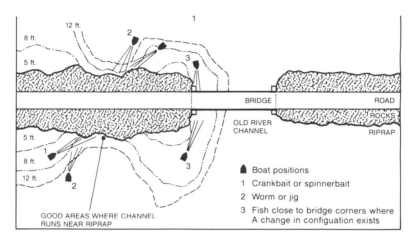

FIGURE 10—*Fishing a current, due to a dropping water level, requires an adjustment in strategy. Bass on the sharper drops are less affected by the change and should be sought.*

The current was sweeping the worm by quickly and it was hard to detect the strikes."

"I was trying to feel the worm in the current and all of a sudden, I would realize that the bass had it and catch one," he says. "I missed about a dozen bass that day there because it was hard to fish the strong current. I was fishing a slip-sinker rig but should have probably been using an exposed hook rig."

Martin, using his electric motor, was holding his boat in the current and casting 'upstream' to the sandbar. He placed his boat on the backside of the sandbar where an eddy was formed. As his offering was washed off the bar into the eddy, bass would strike. Although he missed several hits, the professional did catch a heavy limit that day.

"You can find that situation one day and go back the next and there won't be hardly any current," adds Martin. "You might find a strong current and go back just two hours later and find none. Hydroelectric power plants can generate currents until they stop, and then the current will quit."

When it comes to water level changes, the bass always know what to do. A few anglers, like Tommy Martin, can figure out the effects of a rapid change on bass and continue to catch them.

CHAPTER 10

TEMPERATURE DIFFERENCES

Adjusting To Frontal Cold

STABLE WEATHER often motivates bass to be in a cooperative mood. Decreasing water pH in the fall allows them to move shallow and remain there until cold weather sets in.

The first cold front of the winter, if severe, may be a shock to bass, unprepared for the occurrence. Slight thermal variations have 'lulled' them into complacency. They are still inhabiting gentle sloping flats and shallow cover. They can turn on to the cooling effect or abruptly lose interest in foraging after the front moves through. That makes conditions tougher.

George Cochran, Larry Nixon, Woo Daves, and Rick Clunn are exposed to such conditions during the course of their average 200 days on the water each year. Sooner or later, each will have to figure out a productive fall or winter pattern for foiling a few largemouth, just after the seasons' initial cold front.

Technique and lure variations are required to be successful then. Some methods produce and others do not. These anglers usually have the knowledge to figure out the best moves for the 'lockjaw' problems accompanying a cold front.

George Cochran fishes tournaments throughout the country as well as those near his home in North Little Rock, Arkansas. He spends enough days on the water to be very familiar with cold fronts. The first one of each year is like many others that follow, contends the pro.

"When you are catching fish in a particular area in the late fall and the weather gets bad, that's cause for concern," says Cochran. "You are not able to catch fish as easily."

"What it does is put the fish into the cover," he explains. "About the only way to catch bass then is to flip in the bushes. If you have been catching them in heavy cover, move in on it."

Cochran recommends fishing slower with worms and jigs after the front. He'll also stay longer in one place, working it thoroughly. The effects of that first, harsh cold front on angling success can be improved by moving in tighter on cover (as the bass do), if he has the bass located prior to the weather change.

Larry Nixon, who has met with great success on several tournament trails, has often been faced with frontal conditions. To become one of the country's best all-around bass anglers, he has had to relay on knowledge gained through personal experience.

Feeding Triggers

"The first cold front usually triggers bass to start the fall feeding

The author feels that lure selection is critical depending on the timing of the cold front. He'll pick a crankbait initially and go to a worm or jig when the bass move inside cover.

frenzy," says Nixon. "It starts the water temperature dropping to a more comfortable range. I fish whatever cover a lake has to offer, and this time of year bass are relocating close to deeper water."

On windy days after the front, he likes to use spinnerbaits or crankbaits. The bass are normally very active early in the fall, and Nixon feels that you can also fish better and more effectively with a lure that moves.

After the front has passed and the wind dies, he has noticed the fish will usually go inside the cover. Fish then are hard to catch, and flippin' a jig or worm into the heart of the cover may be the only thing that will work."

"Still, an angler must remember the main consideration in locating bass, and that is cover or structure," Nixon stresses. "If there is a shortage of shallow cover, they have to be on some type of offshore structure. Crankbaits work well there to locate key feeding spots."

"A good front sometimes will put a school of fish on these deeper holes," says Nixon. "Spoons, worms, jigs and grubs produce well, once you locate a honey hole."

Two Types Of Fronts

Woo Daves, from Chester, Virginia, is a frequent placer in top money tournaments around the country. Daves sees usually two types of cold fronts during a year.

"The first is in the spring when you have had warm weather for a period of time, and as surely as there is a tournament, there will be a drop in temperature the day before," he laughs. "The second cold front is in the fall when the temperature seems to drop overnight."

"In the fall, usually you start having mild temperature drops; then, all of a sudden, you get the major drop and it seems to taper off."

Whether it's a spring or fall cold front, though, Daves says the same techniques apply.

"You have to slow down at first," he advises. "Sometimes, this is hard to do, but you have to mentally prepare yourself. When you have been used to fishing at high speed and a bad front drops in, you have to adjust immediately."

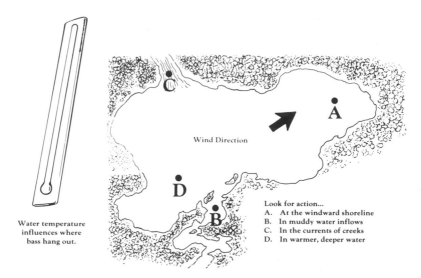

Water temperature influences where bass hang out.

Wind Direction

Look for action...
A. At the windward shoreline
B. In muddy water inflows
C. In the currents of creeks
D. In warmer, deeper water

FIGURE 11—*During cold fronts, bass can still be found. Finding warmer water temperatures usually means more active fish.*

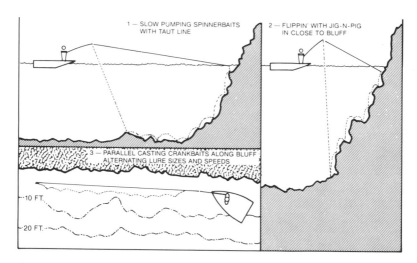

1 — SLOW PUMPING SPINNERBAITS WITH TAUT LINE

2 — FLIPPIN' WITH JIG-N-PIG IN CLOSE TO BLUFF

3 — PARALLEL CASTING CRANKBAITS ALONG BLUFF ALTERNATING LURE SIZES AND SPEEDS

10 FT.

20 FT.

FIGURE 12—*Woo Daves has several rules for catching bass after a front has moved through. Three options would include these.*

"The first rule after a severe cold front hits is to slow the lure down, the second rule is to slow it down some more, and the third rule is to slow it even more! Now you're getting close to retrieving a lure slow enough."

Fish seem to hold really tight to cover and it is ever so important to work structure thoroughly, closely and slowly. You have to present your lure seemingly on the bass' nose to get him to strike, according to Daves. Bass won't move far to take a lure, and that's one reason a flipper seems to really excel during cold front conditions. It's probably the best technique to work an area thoroughly.

When fishing severe cold front conditions, 80 percent of the time Daves will use the flipping method to work a jig or worm right down in the cover tightest to the log, or into the middle of a brushpile. This has been more productive than any other method for him.

Recorder Magic

"The second pattern in cold front conditions is to turn your X-16 on and start looking for drops," he says. "Fish are generally not in a feeding mood during a bad cold front and will hold right on drops or ledges. I will fish these areas with a crankbait, crank it down fast to get the depth, and then slow it down to a crawl. If this doesn't work, I will fish a jig and pig or spinner bait very slowly."

When fishing structure on drops during a cold front, Daves will select a longer rod than normal and lighter line, sometimes eight pound test, to get the lure down deeper. If a crankbait gets down a little deeper, that allows the angler to work it a little slower.

"Another very important thing to remember," says Daves, "is concentration. During severe cold front conditions, it is more important than at any other time. You have to face the reality that you and everyone else are going to get less bites than under normal conditions, and you must make each one count. Remember, many tournaments at that time of year are won with two fish."

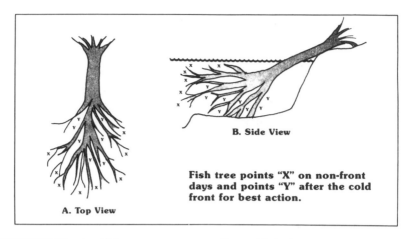

A. Top View

B. Side View

Fish tree points "X" on non-front days and points "Y" after the cold front for best action.

FIGURE 13—*A cold front pattern is normally established early by Daves. Around structure, bass will reposition themselves.*

Positive/Negative Effects

Rick Clunn, three-time Classic champion, is himself a study in concentration. His ability to dedicate every movement toward catching 'little green fish' is well known, and being able to adjust to cold fronts is definitely among his capabilities.

"The first cold front of the fall actually has a positive effect on fishing, as opposed to the negative effect of one in the late fall, winter, or early spring," says Clunn. "Its cooling effect on the water and its signaling of the oncoming winter, actually cause the fish to become much more aggressive and active about feeding."

The bass professional feels that the only possible deterrent to the activity might be excessive wind. That wouldn't hurt the fishing, only hinder an angler's ability to fish, according to Clunn. He has found that after the front, bass will group more. The reduced fall fishing pressure, due to those anglers that hunt or watch sports on TV, has an added positive effect on his ability to concentrate on post-frontal fishing.

The rear one-third areas of major creeks and coves are clunn's favorite places to fish in the fall. Those areas are prime for tossing small crankbaits and spinnerbaits of various sizes. He prefers to use

Concentration is the key to catching more lock-jaw bass after the front, according to Rick Clunn. That fact seems to often allow him to be in the winner's circle at prestigious fall events.

the crankbait along the old creek channels in depths ranging from one to eight feet, on the lip of the creek.

Clunn switches to a spinnerbait where the cover gets thicker and also to fish shallow cover away from the creek channel. His third alternative is flipping a 5/16-ounce Stanley jig and frog into the thickest cover along a shallow channel, when the front is a particularly bad one.

When the weather conditions are constant, you can figure out the bass and go out and catch them the same way, day after day. But when a front is approaching, you have to closely monitor the weather and hope that the bass will open their mouths!

CHAPTER 11

WIND STRENGTHS

Gales Provide A Particular Challenge

HIGH WINDS have been known to wreck havoc with established patterns. They are consistently responsible for bass movement, rough boating conditions and angler frustration.

Not everyone hates the wind, though. Many professional fishermen have learned to extract their bounty from the teeth of a gale. For example, during four days of extremely high winds, Ken Cook won Super BASS I on Florida's St. Johns River. He attributes his success on wind-blown waters there, and elsewhere, to the wave action stirring up sediments and food sources for small organisms.

"Bass are drawn to the area for the food," says Cook. "They can feed there with confidence because of the 'cover' of waves and/or muddied water. Over the years, I've noticed that bass on exposed banks seem to be turned on by wind and wave action."

Ron Shearer agrees. "The wind is a good thing," he says. "It's a lot easier to catch fish with some wind blowing across an area than with none."

George Cochran also believes that wind on a big lake is always a factor. The Classic angler most familiar with the wide Arkansas River contends that wind makes the bass fishing better, if you know what to look for at a particular time of year. White caps are not foreign to many tournament sites that Cochran and other touring pros have visited.

Anchor Dragging

Bass waters don't come any larger than Lake Okeechobee in South Florida, and the wind velocity can increase quickly in those parts. Shearer was undaunted by spring gales during the one invitational tournament held there.

"I managed to catch a limit of bass in the tournament that day when the wind happened to come up on us," he explains. "I dragged four anchors and the boat was still moving fast through the area. The fish were there, though, and I knew it."

Shearer's effective technique was simple. He threw the worm out as far as he could in front of the boat. While drifting toward the bait, he reeled up the slack and set the hook hard.

The Hardin, Kentucky pro admits that it is very difficult to hold the boat in high winds in order to catch bass. Shearer has found, though, that it is quite possible to pull a lot of fish from the wind-blown environment. Dragging two or three anchors and flippin' the grass beds in natural lakes has been a very productive technique for him.

"To be successful at this type of fishing you have to know where the bass are beforehand, though," stresses Shearer. "There's no way you can effectively find bass in this type cover with a high wind blowing."

Baitfish Collection

Larry Williams feels that water movement holds the key to effectively catch wind-blown bass. In such weather conditions, he'll be

Ron Shearer often selects a heavy plastic bait to toss during high winds. Then, he'll drop up to four anchors to slow the boat's drift.

on the lookout for places that may collect baitfish.

A cut into a creek from a shallow bay is an ideal spot during high winds. The northern bassman believes that, although you can toss most lure types and catch fish from the cuts, you must bring it out with the current.

"The wind will blow water into a large bay, which will create a current washing out of the cut into the channel," says Williams. "These areas are better if the current is washing out of shallows, since they usually possess a higher food content."

The pro likes to fish bridge areas, seawall breaks, even culverts with the wind blowing into them. He advises not to be afraid of fishing the windy shorelines and points. Williams prefers lures that most closely imitate the baitfish that are being blown up on the banks. That's what the bass are accustomed to seeing during this foraging.

Tommy Martin also chooses between spinnerbaits, crankbaits and buzzbaits when fishing during high winds. Worms or jigs require "feel", and Martin is aware of the difficulty in detecting strikes during high winds. The wind and wave action most always make the bass more active, according to the Texan.

Windy flats with underwater vegetation such as hydrilla or milfoil can be good, according to Martin. Rocky points or points with underwater stumps are also good places to catch bass when the wind is blowing in on them. He looks for rip rap rock, underwater shoals, or small humps out in the lake during high winds. The key element on the topography must be cover of some type.

"Small pockets or coves just off the main lake are good when the wind is blowing into them. The wind blows plankton into these areas and the shad feed on the plankton," he adds. "The wind makes the bass in that area active, and they feed on the shad. They'll chase lures well too!"

Tight-Line Lures

Ken Cook's lure selection in high winds is also well defined. In windy weather, he fishes with the more practical, tight-line lures, such as spinnerbaits or crankbaits. When casting drop baits, such as worms or jigs, into the wind, difficulties can arise.

"My favorite is spinnerbaits, but the lure choice should be dictated by cover-type more than any other single thing," says Cook. "For instance, I use spinnerbaits in weeds, reeds, moss, brush, trees, etc., to minimize hangups. If the bank is fairly obstruction-free, I'll more likely use a crankbait that matches size and type of available food."

Cook will fish all points with a little bit of current to help position feeding fish. And he'll be on the windy banks, regardless of how rough it is. The limiting factor to "how windy is too windy" to fish those spots is, according to the multi-tournament winner, "when the boat sinks."

Cochran determines which points to fish during high winds by the time of year. In the spring, the fish will be in the coves. The wind will 'pull' the bass out onto the points and windy banks in the cove.

"The bass will be in dingier water just behind the points looking for bait fish," says Cochran. "Sometimes they're in the calm water, just out of the wind. And in the summer, they are on the main lake points and dingy banks."

Clarity Considerations

Shearer notes that waters that are extremely clear require special consideration. The best factor for fishing in the wind, according to the burly pro, is finding a wind-blown shoreline, especially on a clear lake. The shore is being 'stirred up' and a mud ring develops.

"Once the muddy water appears, that signals bass that forage are being washed out of rocks," says Shearer. "Hence, a jig or crayfish-colored crankbait is very effective."

Fishing the sides of points in a high wind is an extremely good pattern for him also. The wind sets up a lot of current around the points, and a mud ring is often pushed along.

"Bass will hold behind these points and move up in the low visibility waters to feed," says Shearer. "They will usually go around the point and feed just off the breakers. That is an excellent jig or crankbait pattern."

When the wind direction is perpendicular to a bridge, the current is forced through the pilings. Forage is then washed through the

Preferring tight-line lures when working wind-blown areas, Ken Cook's selection criteria depends on the amount of structure present and its density.

bridge area, which attracts the bass . . . and Shearer. Wind will blow schools of shad around and wash crayfish out of shoreline rocks. He is extremely partial to a good wind.

"About the only exception is in the spring, when I'm fishing cold, muddy water. That's the worst time to try to catch fish and I certainly don't want a wind then," says Shearer. "I want it to be still so that the shallow water is allowed to warm up quicker. Once the water warms, the baitfish will become active, and so will the bass."

Jerk And Hook

On extremely clear waters buffeted by high winds, Williams relies on a 'jerk' technique to fool bass. A bright sun makes his method of fishing large Rapalas over wide, three-to-eight-foot deep flats even more deadly.

"When I say jerk, I mean jerk it as hard as you can," says Williams. "I'll jerk the Rapala for perhaps 10 to 15 feet and then suddenly stop it. Then, just wiggle your rod tip for a second. This will generally get you the strike. If not, start jerking and stop it again."

Williams prefers the larger size Rapalas. By drifting with the wind and throwing downwind with a spinning rod and 10 pound test, he can cast an amazing distance even with the Rapala. The yankee basser can cover a lot of area in a short time.

"If you'll stop and think about it, it's an area that very few people are fishing," explains Williams. "Most people are either fishing the bank or out on the sharp dropoff, on one extremity of the flat."

The professionals are often faced with high winds during the course of several consecutive tournament days on the water. Many have learned to adapt to windy conditions which would normally drive the rest of us off the water. They have had to, though. Money was on the line.

CHAPTER 12

OFF-STRUCTURE MOVEMENT

Locating Suspended Largemouth

ANGLERS OFTEN CURSE their favorite quarry when it's not to be found beside the tree trunk or under the canopy of floating vegetation. A careful investigation of all other structure in both shallow and deep water reveals nothing. The lure tossers now become very angry.

Had there been a big fish kill that escaped the local papers? Where are the fish?

Not to despair, they can be found and some can even be caught. The suspended bass is among the lowliest of all critters alright, but that reputation can be quickly altered with a few tugs on the end of the mono.

There are specific reasons why bass suspend. Water level fluctuations, low dissolved oxygen, cold fronts and falling barometric pressures, or unfavorable water chemistry factors such as pH levels, can move or redistribute the largemouth.

Seasonal environmental changes that modify the water quality and quantity affect bass migrations. The rapid redistribution of fish, including that of forage, can occur most any time during the year, but suspended bass are most often found in the summer, fall and winter months.

The period during which largemouth move from established territories and home ranges on a particular lake or river may depend on weather. Excessive run-off or rainfall may suddenly alter the pH of the water. Few anglers keep up with the day-to-day changes that lakes and their fisheries go through, but plenty experience them.

The touring professionals make a living out of figuring out bass and their behavior as influenced by various factors. Suspended largemouth are one potential problem that the successful anglers frequently have to deal with.

Two Types Of Suspension

Randy Fite points out that there are two different kinds of suspended bass; the first kind are those that suspend off structure. You can find this type situation in existence maybe nine months a year. Catching them is usually difficult.

"My answer to that condition is to keep looking for fish that are more bottom-oriented or related," he admits. "They are easier fish to catch."

The other situation arises when the dissolved oxygen in the depths becomes depleted, and the fish will suspend shallower where they can find a higher concentration of oxygen. Fite has found these

Randy Fite often finds bass suspended in high oxygen areas above waters void of dissolved oxygen. They are usually scattered though, so he covers more water to find them.

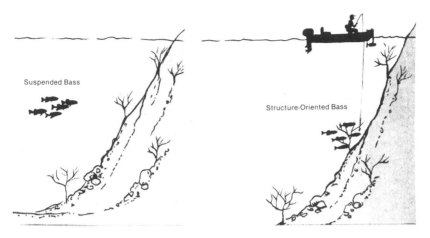

FIGURE 14—*Bass that are suspended are harder to locate and catch than those relating to some kind of structure. Many will ultimately move horizontally to orient around structure.*

fish to be very catchable.

Fish suspended in the high oxygen areas tend to spread out; deep, suspended fish are even more scattered. You just have to cover more water to find them, according to Fite.

Another potential problem he has encountered is that bass are not as dependable—they aren't necessarily at the same spot the next day. Suspended fish tend to be more migratory than those relating to a bush on the bottom, for example. The suspended bass will probably be in the same area but not at the same spot.

Are all suspended bass extremely hard to catch? Fite doesn't think so. It depends on the depth at which they are holding, according to the deep water expert. That can be determined from a chart recorder.

You should be seeing suspended fish below 15 feet, according to Fite. If not, the oxygen, pH or something else has caused the fish to move above that level. In such a case, you can check that range out with a variety of lures. A crankbait is Fite's preferred selection.

"If the fish are below 15 feet, I'll find them with my recorder or LCR," says Fite. "Those kind of fish are hard to catch because it is difficult to keep a lure at that precise depth. It's much easier to keep a lure on the bottom, which may be 30 feet in this case."

On the deep fish, Fite will generally chart an area and then use his LCR with trolling motor-mounted transducer to locate individual bass or small clusters. He will then reposition himself over those fish and vertical-jig a spoon or lead-headed grub.

Overfishing Contact Points

Ron Shearer has, in his travels, found numerous suspended bass. When the bass are suspended in open water at the same depth as the contact point of the structure that they're using, then it's possible to catch them, according to the bassman.

"I developed a technique called overfishing of points," he says. "You stay back off the point and cast across it. Then, pull your boat up on the center of the point, backing away from the contact point."

"For example, if there's a stump in 12-foot of water that the bass are coming in on, set your boat in six foot of water and fan cast into the water around the point," he explains. "Bass suspended at 12 foot below the surface will be getting ready to migrate in to feed around the stump, or will have just quit."

Either way, Shearer figures that those fish located at the same depth as the contact point are catchable. Schools of bass will often suspend shallower, however, requiring them to descend in order to reach their contact point. The Kentuckian finds such fish very difficult to catch.

Catching suspended fish is directly related to where they are on the structure, according to Shearer. In the spring, when bass are in the bushes on Kentucky Lake, where he lives, everyone catches fish.

"If a cold front comes through, the bass will move out into the back of the bays in five to seven foot of water on scattered stumps. They're not schooled up and each bass will select an individual stump. You can move a boat across them, and with a chart recorder, you can see the bass beside the stumps."

Luring Dormant Fish

"You can idle across them and throw back and catch every fish," Shearer notes. "If the bass suspend on top of the stump, though, you

FIGURE 15—*Some means of reading the depth is necessary to find suspended bass.*

just cannot catch them. Ninety percent of the bass that are suspended are also dormant most of the time. You may be able to see them, but you can't catch them."

"You can jig over the top of them with a jigging spoon and hit them, but never catch them," says Shearer. "I've sat on top of a school of 100 bass like this before."

There are times when bass refuse to feed, and anglers have to learn to accept that when fishing for suspended fish. When bass are suspended at the same depth as the contact point, an angler is lucky enough to catch them seven times out of ten, according to Shearer.

A good angler can determine that contact point by mapping every piece of the structure they're using with a chart recorder, and by looking at every little break or piece of structure on the structure. Bass will often be on the structure closest to the deepest water.

The best place to find a concentration of bass is the contact point where the fish first come in from open water, according to Shearer. They will spread out from that point into the shallows in search of food. Although you may catch two by a log near the bank, he figures that there will be more fish on the deep-water stump (contact point) during the feeding period than anywhere else.

Water Fluctuation Push

Gary Klein, born and raised in California, learned how to fish the man-made, water supply reservoirs that fluctuate every day. The normal fluctuation of his home reservoir is 95 feet a year. Bass there are always off the bank due to that, according to Klein. The erosion that occurs from the significant fluctuations also tends to wipe out any shore cover and move fish out from the banks.

"If the bass are suspended off bottom, they are there for a reason—and that reason is not good," he says. "They are not relating to anything. The problem that most of us have is that we usually let our lures go to the bottom, so in this case, we're fishing below the fish."

Klein's favorite technique to catch suspended bass is 'doodling', a unique way of shaking the worm. He fishes four-inch worms off the bottom with spinning outfits and six-pound test line.

"I used the technique on Georgia's Lake Sidney Lanier and placed third in a major tournament," says Klein. "I was catching 30 to 60 spotted bass each day in 35 feet of water and they were all

Bass will follow forage to open water and suspend below them for long periods. The author has found a crankbait that resembles the threadfin shad to be very productive on such fish.

suspended off the bottom. My partners were dragging worms along the bottom and having a rough time."

At a major tournament on Lake Meade, the professional found bass suspended off deep points. The water was clear and warm, so the fish were very aggressive. They move a lot when their metabolism is high. The bass were relating to points but were out over deeper water.

The points coming out could be seen with a good pair of sunglasses. Klein would follow the reefs on out to where he figured, from past experience, they would break. Then, he would doodle with the light line and small worm.

"I would make the cast in front of me and give it slack line, so that the worm was chasing the slip sinker down vertically," says Klein. "I would shake the line with the rod tip as the worm fell. The slip sinker would move up against the worm and the rig would spiral down," he explains. "Almost every one of my fish ate it on the fall, in 30 to 50 feet of water."

Such a technique is an effective method to cover water quickly. The young bass pro pitches the bait out, strips out a bunch of line, and lets the worm go down 25 or 30 feet. Then, he'll start shaking it. Since Klein was probably the only angler in a field of 252 to catch four daily limits, he figures that the technique works well on suspended fish.

Sometimes, you can beat the banks to death and not find fish, yet go out from shore and find them stacked up. Then, you might catch a limit in 15 or 20 minutes. Fishing for suspended bass is often like that. It's either feast or famine!

CHAPTER 13

TOPOGRAPHY VARIATIONS

Point Perfection Along The Contours

POINTS EXIST in all shapes, sizes and materials . . . just like fishing lures. They can be formed by vegetation, rock, sand or mud for example. To bass, these topographical variations mean excellent ambush places.

The largemouth bass is one of the world's most efficient predators. He is adept at lurking in shadows and "pouncing" on any hapless forage that swims too close. He uses topography to his advantage, and points are a vital link in the game plan.

Some points are obvious; others are not. All are generally productive, since they offer a change in either cover or depth. Most anglers can spot the long sloping point at the confluence of two tributaries. But few realize that even submerged weed beds can offer points. Those that do often can catch several largemouth without moving the boat.

There are a variety of methods that may be employed to effectively fish points. Anyone who has spent a lot of time on the water has developed different techniques to use, depending on various conditions. For example, I've found that determining the pH breakline (where the pH value changes substantially in a foot or two of depth) and then fishing across the point at that depth helps me locate more bass.

Less sophisticated methods equally as effective can be utilized, based on experience. Better bass anglers are able to analyze the surface expression of the point and make a determination of the best technique. Submerged points are usually inspected by depth finders.

Tommy Martin's experience confirms that points are some of the most productive areas on all lakes. The expert is familiar with fishing several types of points.

Points come in a variety of configurations and most attract the largemouth. A depth finder is often needed to find submerged points. Lures should be worked parallel to the orientation of the primary cover or drop-off.

Grass Points

During the summer, grass points in a river-type lake such as Chickamauga, near Chattanooga, Tennessee, is a favorite of Martin's. They produce lots of bass, as he and I found out one August. The best pattern during our day's outing was using a spinnerbait around the grass points. We caught over 30 largemouth from six or eight points. Unfortunately, few met the legal weigh-in size minimum of 12 inches.

"I like to fish the cuts that are made through the grass, like we did today," he told me. "The creek channels that come out through the grass beds and hit the main river channel form points that are always productive."

Once the current starts moving, a lot of baitfish are attracted to the these grassy points. In turn, the baitfish attract bass. On grass points in five to eight feet of water, Martin prefers to use spinnerbaits, topwater lures or buzz baits. All can be very effective.

"Plastic worms are always going to be effective on points too," says Martin. "I've found that a little grub with eight pound test line and spinning tackle can be very productive in such places. A lot of the bass that bunch up on points of grass are not necessarily big bass, though. As we found out, points attract little bass too."

"A lot of grass grows in eight or 10 feet of water depending on how clear the water may be, and the points can be very good," he says. "In the winter months, I'll vertically jig these points with a jig and plastic trailer."

The points of grass that seem to be so good on the shallow bodies of water are extremely long, extending for hundreds of yards into the lake. Those beds of vegetation form the first type of cover that the bass will migrate into from the main lake, and there is usually adequate water depth.

Submerged hydrilla forms some of the better grass points, but they can be found only by using electronics. Thus, a lot of anglers won't find them. Everyone can see the visible points of grass that run out into the lake and they will fish them. The ones under the water, though, are really "honey holes."

"I established a pattern on the St. Johns River in Florida fishing big points of reed beds," says Martin. "When the wind was blowing into these points, the baitfish would soon come in and then the bass."

Several bass attacked his tandem-blade spinnerbait as he retrieved the lure back quickly to make the surface bulge. The largemouth, averaging two to three pounds, would strike at the bait vigorously. They hardly ever missed it.

Timber Points

Timber points are also great places for bass to hold, particularly in the fall. The timber lines in 15 to 25 feet of the water are very good, and their points are particularly good if there is a break in the bottom structure on or near the point. For instance, a 15-foot deep hump right on the point with water 25 feet deep all around the point is ideal.

Points where creek channels come out of the timber and intersect with the open water are some of the better areas for fall and winter fishing. Wooded points are also good bets for summer bass, and Martin opts to fish the plastic worm during the hotter months. During cooler times, he'll most often use a jig and pig and fish it vertically.

A key to finding the better points in the summer, fall and winter is to watch for blue herons. They'll sit in the trees on points and await the arrival of schools of threadfin shad. Bass will occasionally drive the shad to the surface and that's why the herons are there.

Two or three extremely alert herons sitting on a timber point should let you know that bass have been driving shad to the top in that area. The bass should still be present on that particular point.

Rocky Points

Points of rock or boulders offer a different form of bass-holding structure. Martin normally catches more fish off rocky points in the

FIGURE 16—*Wooded points are prime haunts for bass. Bass can be using the shallows during spring time and low-light conditions, and they can be found on the deeper wood-laden edges during other times of the year.*

110

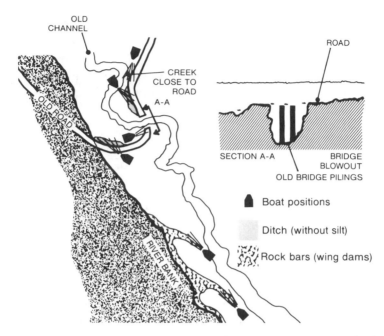

FIGURE 17—*Rocky points are often found along rivers, sometimes in the form of "wing walls," and along inundated road beds near submerged creek channels.*

spring than at any other time of the year. These points are very good Kentucky or spotted bass hangouts in most of the midwest and southern lakes.

"I catch most fish off rocky points by throwing deep diving crankbaits," he says. "I'll use a crawfish or Tennessee shad-colored bait. Often the fish will be on the sides of the rocky points or at a location wherever cover is available on the point. Often many of these points have stump cover on them."

"I like a long, sloping point that runs out 50 yards or so into the lake," explains Martin. "The little short, steep points don't seem to produce as well. One with big rocks near shore that has deep water on both sides is best."

On the much better points, there are usually eight or 10 feet of water depth. They are especially productive if there are big chunk rock and a few stumps along them. Deep running crankbaits fished alongside these points are tremendously effective in the spring months.

Although Martin's number one lure on rocky points is a crankbait, he can usually catch bass on a worm or the jig and frog. If the points are shallow enough and the spring time cover is near the surface, he'll use spinnerbaits or buzz baits.

Cranking rocky points is easy. In the spring, when the water temperature is on a warming trend and between 55 and 62 degrees, bass are usually very aggressive. They will chase fast moving crankbaits, so the successful angler will generally crank the bait at a medium to fast speed. Try both speeds.

Many anglers prefer to use fairly light line if the cover on the rocky points is not particularly dense. Martin will opt for 10 or 12 pound test monofilament to allow his crankbait to run deeper and make contact with the bottom. It's very important to bump the rocks and stumps to make noise and attract bass.

They'll often hit the crankbait just after the bump. Any time that the bait makes an irregular jump, such as when it pops free from a rock or stump, it may initiate a strike.

I can't remember having more fun than when I was crashing a Norman Big N through flooded trees off a point. The lure was hung up occasionally, but more often than not, the dive was stopped by a largemouth. Most of the dozen or so bass hit after the lure was bumped into a tree.

Mud And Sand Points

Sandy points frequently will not have a lot of cover on them. They are usually located on the upper end of lakes where the water is primarily into the main river and creek channels.

Sandbar points are prime spinnerbait or buzzbait areas. You need some kind of cover on those points, though, to hold bass for very long. On river-type lakes, sandbars that come out from the shores may be numerous. Those points will often stop logs drifting downstream, and such places are great for bass.

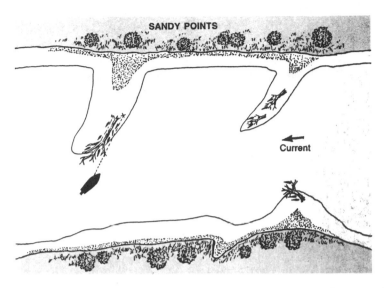

FIGURE 18—*River sand bars often collect logs and other debris that is washed into them via currents. The super bass-attracting cover is best fished by casting parallel to the "blow-downs."*

Mud points are also found up the rivers into the smaller tributaries. Logs are frequently buried on the edges of mud flats, and again that's where the bass will be found. When the watersheds get a lot of rainfall and the water level gets high, brush will often become lodged on the mud flats and partially buried.

Logs 12 or 14 inches in diameter and 40 feet long or so are prime bass holding areas on mud flat points. You can find these by using and correctly interpreting your depthfinder. A mud bottom will show up as a very solid or narrow reading while a harder bottom will be depicted as a thicker reading.

Martin has found these topographical variations to be productive bass spots under most conditions. Regardless of the type-point, they can be effectively worked. We both usually head for them first, and the bass nearly always beat us there.

CHAPTER 14

VEGETATION HABITATS

Finding The Bass-Holding Weeds

YOU'VE SEEN IT, the state agency's aquatic 'weed control' boat cruising the shallows spraying every bit of green in sight. Then for days, the fishing stinks. And if they're real effective, the fishing never really comes back. They think that most weeds in a watery environment are bad. 'They' are wrong.

Most aquatic vegetation is valuable to a bass fishery, and the anglers that are out on the water 250 days a year are well aware of that. The professional fishermen that travel the country are probably most cognizant of the fact that vegetation often receives an undeserved bad rap. Those anglers know how to separate the "scales from the weed" and derive the maximum benefit from such.

Denny Brauer agrees that weeds are a definite advantage in most lakes. They offer good cover for all species and help the food chain system. Weeds also help strain the silt out of water and help the water quality of a body of water. He believes that aquatic vegetation is often an advantage in lakes, except those extremely shallow bodies of water that become completely choked.

"Weeds are an advantage to the fishermen; they can help position and concentrate bass to make them easier to locate and pattern," points out Brauer.

Of all weeds, his favorite type is reeds, due to the fact that they can be fished very effectively. Bass usually like the edges, and reeds have a very definite edge.

Irregularities

"You can pattern bass on reed lines according to the irregular features, points, pockets, heavy clumps, matted reeds, etc." Brauer says. "A deeper stretch of reeds will usually hold the larger bass. Also any piece of wood or other object in the reeds is an added bonus. Places where clumps of reeds have been broken down and matted by muskrats and beavers can also be big bass magnets."

Brauer has found bullrushes can also be excellent bass habitat, but are tougher to fish. The fact that they don't form a definite edge line makes them more difficult to pattern. Both reeds and bullrushes are very tough-stemmed, and getting big fish out of them can be difficult.

The flippin' method is usually the best way for Brauer to pull bass from those weeds. In the case of extremely clear water and/or spooky fish, he'll stay back and pitch a worm or a jig and frog into the cover. Spoons, spinnerbaits, and topwaters can also be productive.

Brauer feels that a combination of weeds is usually a bonus. An example would be where peppergrass and coontail or hydrilla are intermingled. Bass prefer different types of weeds at different times of the year, and even at different times of the day, according to the frequent tournament winner.

"They may be feeding in grass beds in front of a reed line early in the morning and then move back into the reeds during the day," says Brauer. "The brighter the skies the tighter bass will be to the weeds."

"Fish the dark spots," he advises. "Peppergrass beds are great areas to toss spoons and topwater lures. They also can be fished by using the wind to blow your boat through them. Flip the holes in the grass as you drift along."

Milfoil and hydrilla are great cover in deeper lakes, according to Brauer. He has seen it grow to depths of up to 30 feet depending on water clarity. Both can be a problem in real shallow lakes and can choke them out. That will ruin the balance of the lake.

"When these weeds are submerged, good fish can be caught by jerking a Ripp'n Minnow or Rapala over the top of them," says Brauer. "This method is best in the cooler times and seasons. When they grow to the top and mat, you can work spoons and weedless surface baits over the cover."

In warmer seasons, he prefers a worm or jig and frog worked almost vertically with short pitches along the deep edges. By pitch-

Inaccessibility due to dense vegetation is what protects some of the lunker bass from year-round pressure. Those anglers that know how to fish it do well, though.

ing the lure and shaking it while trying to leave it in one spot, the fish will be drawn to the bait.

Enemy Lists

Rick Clunn's favorite type of weeds for largemouth bass are hydrilla, milfoil and coontail moss.

"Obviously, the first two are on every state's weed control authority's Number One enemy list," says Clunn. "That's unfortunate, because hydrilla is literally a fish factory. A lake of 5,000 acres or more with hydrilla is impossible to fish out."

Clunn is most familiar with hydrilla because thousands of acres of it existed at one time in his home waters, Lake Conroe. He found the survival rate of yearling bass to be extraordinary. The Texas angler also determined that the fish seemed to occupy more area of the lake due to the increased habitat provided.

"It is my opinion that a lake with hydrilla can, and will, support at least four times the amount of bass than it would without it. Admittedly, hydrilla is sometimes hard to fish and it does make some areas of a lake inaccessible at certain times of the year," he adds, "but this inaccessibility is also what protects the fish from year-round fishing pressure."

Hydrilla makes for an excellent topwater lake, according to Clunn. Buzzbaits, chuggers, and stick baits are his favorites. A jig and eel is also excellent year around in hydrilla due to the weed's coarse nature. A quick jerk usually clears the jig of weeds.

Clunn's favorite method is to cast a 9/16 ounce Stanley jig parallel to the deeper edges in 10 to 20 feet of water. He'll make very short pitches ahead of the boat and fish the bait mostly vertically. Then he will simply shake the jig until it falls down through the holes in the weed bed.

Bass Thickets

Harold Allen asks, "How many times have we found an area of matted grass, weeds, milfoil, or other type of vegetation and passed it up? Upon studying the situation, we use the excuse it will take too long to work it out, or I couldn't get a lure back through it, or if I got a hit I couldn't get him out."

"These are the same places that, if we sit there a while, we would start to hear the bluegill smack while feeding, black birds light on the thicker patches of grass, or the sudden unmistakable sound of a big bass way back in the stuff."

"Some of the best trophies ever taken weren't trophies strictly for their size," he says. "A lot of times the terrain is just as big a challenge as the animal itself. Understanding too that a trophy from the weeds is a personal achievement and not always a record size of the species sets the stage for some exciting hunting, or in this case, fishing."

Allen notes there are several ways to fish dense, matted vegetation; every one of them require precise lure placement, nerves of steel, and always heavy tackle.

"People might say it's not very sporting to fish for small bass with 30 pound test line. Match your gear to the occasion," he says. "To me, it's not very sporting to break off three feet of line in a fish's mouth."

The easiest way to fish heavy vegetation may be by flipping the outside. The only problem is if the fish aren't active or moving around, they won't be close to the outside. Allen believes that a big tail 5- or 6-inch worm will usually do the trick, though.

"When fishing large areas of dense matted vegetation, always watch for movement," he says. "Bass moving around under the cover will cause the grass to move around. Listen also for the sound of feeding fish; that's another giveaway."

Weedy Movements

Two methods or lures have worked well for him in these situations. The old frog is still by far the best, he believes. You may miss a lot of strikes, but after the day is over, you know you've been fishing. Another good lure is a large, eight-inch plastic worm with a big curl tail. The worm is most effective when rigged Texas-style without a weight, using a 5/0 or 6/0 hook.

"Both the frog and the worm need to be cast as far back into cover as possible, making sure to work the lure across every small opening on the retrieve," advises Allen. "Work the lure slowly but deliberately, in effect teasing the fish every inch of the way until the lure hits the edge of the opening. Then, look out!"

Allen feels that stiff rods with heavy line are the key to landing bass from the weeds. When the fish hits, he will give slack, then reel

Weeds are the home to many largemouth bass and knowing the best techniques will help put them in the boat. Flippin' is a great method for worming heavy weed cover.

down and set the hook hard. Then, the pro angler holds back on the rod and pulls with as much force as possible.

"It is then or never," says Allen. "The number of fish boated versus the strikes will disappoint you, but," he asks, "do trophies come easy?"

I think that these experienced anglers would agree that aquatic vegetation is desirous in most waters. They have all 'unlocked' the secret to catching what is hidden within and below. It sometimes takes extra effort and patience, but it will pay off for anglers at all skill levels.

BASS SERIES LIBRARY!

Eight Great Books With A Wealth Of Information
For Bass Fishermen

By Larry Larsen

I. FOLLOW THE FORAGE FOR BETTER BASS ANGLING - **VOLUME 1 BASS/PREY RELATIONSHIP** - The most important key to catching bass is finding them in a feeding mood. Knowing the predominant forage, its activity and availability, as well as its location in a body of water will enable an angler to catch more and larger bass. Whether you fish artificial lures or live bait, you will benefit from this book.

SPECIAL FEATURES

o PREDATOR/FORAGE INTERACTION
o BASS FEEDING BEHAVIOR
o UNDERSTANDING BASS FORAGE
o BASS/PREY PREFERENCES
o FORAGE ACTIVITY CHART

II. FOLLOW THE FORAGE FOR BETTER BASS ANGLING - **VOLUME 2 TECHNIQUES** - Beginners and veterans alike will achieve more success utilizing proven concepts that are based on predator/forage interactions. Understanding the reasons behind lure or bait success will result in highly productive, bass-catching patterns.

SPECIAL FEATURES

o LURE SELECTION CRITERIA
o EFFECTIVE PATTERN DEVELOPMENT
o NEW BASS CATCHING TACTICS
o FORAGING HABITAT
o BAIT AND LURE METHODS

III. BASS PRO STRATEGIES - Professional fishermen have opportunities to devote extended amounts of time to analyzing a body of water and planning a productive day on it. They know how changes in pH, water temperature, color and fluctuations affect bass fishing, and they know how to adapt to weather and topographical variations. This book reveals the methods that the country's most successful tournament anglers have employed to catch bass almost every time out. The reader's productivity should improve after spending a few hours with this compilation of techniques!

SPECIAL FEATURES

o MAPPING & WATER ELIMINATION
o LOCATE DEEP & SHALLOW BASS
o BOAT POSITION FACTORS
o WATER CHEMISTRY INFLUENCES
o WEATHER EFFECTS
o TOPOGRAPHICAL TECHNIQUES

IV. BASS LURES - TRICKS & TECHNIQUES - Modifications of lures and development of new baits and techniques continue to keep the fare fresh, and that's important. Bass seem to become "accustomed" to the same artificials and presentations seen over and over again. As a result, they become harder to catch. It's the new approach that again sparks the interest of some largemouth. To that end, this book explores some of the latest ideas for modifying, rigging and using them. The lure modifications, tricks and techniques presented within these covers will work anywhere in the country.

SPECIAL FEATURES

o UNIQUE LURE MODIFICATIONS
o IN-DEPTH VARIABLE REASONING
o PRODUCTIVE PRESENTATIONS
o EFFECTIVE NEW RIGGINGS
o TECHNOLOGICAL ADVANCES

V. SHALLOW WATER BASS - Catching shallow water largemouth is not particularly difficult. Catching lots of them usually is. Even more challenging is catching lunker-size bass in seasons other than during the spring spawn. Anglers applying the information within the covers of this book on marshes, estuaries, reservoirs, lakes, creeks or small ponds should triple their results. The book details productive new tactics to apply to thin-water angling. Numerous photographs and figures easily define the optimal locations and proven methods to catch bass.

SPECIAL FEATURES

o UNDERSTANDING BASS/COVER INTERFACE
o METHODS TO LOCATE BASS CONCENTRATIONS
o ANALYSIS OF WATER TYPES
o TACTICS FOR SPECIFIC HABITATS
o LARSEN'S "FLORA FACTOR"

VI. BASS FISHING FACTS - This angler's guide to the lifestyles and behavior of the black bass is a reference source of sorts, never before compiled. The book explores the behavior of bass during pre- and post-spawn as well as during bedding season. It examines how bass utilize their senses to feed and how they respond to environmental factors. The book details how fishermen can be more productive by applying such knowledge to their bass angling. The information within the covers of this book includes those bass species, known as "other" bass, such as redeye, Suwannee, spotted, etc.

SPECIAL FEATURES

o BASS FORAGING MOTIVATORS
o DETAILED SPRING MOVEMENTS
o A LOOK AT BASS SENSES
o GENETIC INTRODUCTION/STUDIES
o MINOR BASS SPECIES & HABITATS

VII. TROPHY BASS - is focused at today's dedicated lunker hunters who find more enjoyment in wrestling with one or two monster largemouth than with a "panfull" of yearlings. To help the reader better understand how to catch big bass, a majority of this book explores productive techniques for trophies. The "how to" information was gleaned from professional guides and other experienced trophy bass hunters. This book takes a look at the geographical areas and waters that offer better opportunities to catch giant bass.

SPECIAL FEATURES

o GEOGRAPHIC DISTRIBUTIONS
o STATE RECORD INFORMATION
o GENETIC GIANTS
o TECHNIQUES FOR TROPHIES
o LOCATION CONSIDERATIONS
o LURE AND BAIT TIMING

VIII. AN ANGLER'S GUIDE TO BASS PATTERNS examines the most effective combination of lure, method and places. Being able to develop a pattern of successful methods and lures for specific habitats and environmental conditions is the key to catching several bass on each fishing trip. Understanding bass movements and activities and the most appropriate and effective techniques to employ will add many pounds of enjoyment to the sport of bass fishing. "Bass Patterns" is a reference source for all anglers, regardless of where they live or their skill level.

SPECIAL FEATURES

o BOAT POSITIONING
o NEW WATER STRATEGIES
o DEPTH AND COVER CONCEPTS
o MOVING WATER TACTICS
o WEATHER/ACTIVITY FACTORS
o TRANSITIONAL TECHNIQUES

LARSEN'S OUTDOOR PUBLISHING
CONVENIENT ORDER FORM
ALL PRICES INCLUDE POSTAGE/HANDLING

FRESH WATER
____ BSL1. Better Bass Angling Vol 1 ($13.95)
____ BSL2. Better Bass Angling Vol 2 ($13.95)
____ BSL3. Bass Pro Strategies ($13.95)
____ BSL4. Bass Lures/Techniques ($13.95)
____ BSL5. Shallow Water Bass ($13.95)
____ BSL6. Bass Fishing Facts ($13.95)
____ BSL7. Trophy Bass ($13.95)
____ BSL8. Bass Patterns ($13.95)
____ BSL9. Bass Guide Tips ($13.95)
____ CF1. Mstrs' Scrts/Crappie Fshng ($12.45)
____ CF2. Crappie Tactics ($12.45)
____ CF3. Mstr's Secrets of Catfishing ($12.45)
____ LB1. Larsen on Bass Tactics ($15.45)
____ PF1. Peacock Bass Explosions! ($16.95)
____ PF2. Peacock Bass & Other Fierce
              Exotics ($17.95)

SALT WATER
____ IL1. The Snook Book ($13.95)
____ IL2. The Redfish Book ($13.95)
____ IL3. The Tarpon Book ($13.95)
____ IL4. The Trout Book ($13.95)
____ SW1. The Reef Fishing Book ($16.45)

OTHER OUTDOORS BOOKS
____ DL1. Diving to Adventure ($12.45)
____ DL2. Manatees/Vanishing ($11.45)
____ DL3. Sea Turtles/Watchers' ($11.45)
____ OC1. Outdoor Chuckle Book ($9.95)

REGIONAL
____ FG1. Secret Spots-Tampa Bay/
              Cedar Key   ($15.45)
____ FG2. Secret Spots - SW Florida ($15.45)
____ BW1. Guide/North Fl. Waters ($14.95)
____ BW2. Guide/Cntral Fl.Waters ($14.95)
____ BW3. Guide/South Fl.Waters ($14.95)
____ OT1. Fish/Dive - Caribbean   ($11.95)
____ OT3. Fish/Dive Florida/ Keys ($13.95)

HUNTING
____ DH1. Mstrs' Secrets/ Deer Hunting ($13.95)
____ DH2. Science of Deer Hunting ($13.95)
____ DH3. Mstrs' Secrets/Bowhunting ($12.45)
____ DH4. How to Take Monster Bucks ($13.95)
____ TH1. Mstrs' Secrets/ Turkey Hunting ($13.95)
____ OA1. Hunting Dangerous Game! ($9.95)
____ OA2. Game Birds & Gun Dogs ($9.95)
____ BP1. Blackpowder Hunting Secrets ($14.45)

BOOKS & VIDEO SPECIAL
DISCOUNT PACKAGES
____ V1 - Video - Advanced Bass Tactics $29.95
____ BSL - Bass Series Library (9 vol. set) $94.45
____ IL - Inshore Library (4 vol. set) $42.95
____ BW - Guides to Bass Waters (3 vols.) $37.95
Volume sets are autographed by each author.

BIG MULTI-BOOK DISCOUNT!
2-3 books, SAVE 10%
4 or more books, SAVE20%

INTERNATIONAL ORDERS
Send check in U.S. funds; add $6
more per book for airmail rate

ALL PRICES INCLUDE POSTAGE/HANDLING

No. of books _____ x $_____ea =$_____	*Special Package* _____ @ $_____
No. of books _____ x $_____ea =$_____	*Video (50-min) $29.95 = $_____*
Multi-book Discount (%) $_____	*(Pkgs include discount)= N/A*
SUBTOTAL 1 $_____	*SUBTOTAL 2* $_____

_____For Priority Mail (add $2 more per book) $_____
TOTAL   ENCLOSED   (check or money order) $_____

NAME_____ADDRESS_____

CITY_____STATE_____ZIP_____

Send check or Money Order to: Larsen's Outdoor Publishing, Dept. BK-97
2640 Elizabeth Place, Lakeland, FL 33813 (941)644-3381
(Sorry, no credit card orders)